TRILLION DOLLAR BABY

Also by Paul Cleary

Shakedown: Australia's Grab for Timor Oil

The Men Who Came Out of the Ground

Too Much Luck: The Mining Boom and Australia's Future

Mine-Field: The Dark Side of Australia's Resources Rush

TRILLION DOLLAR BABY

HOW NORWAY BEAT THE OIL GIANTS
AND WON A LASTING FORTUNE

PAUL CLEARY

Biteback Publishing

This edition published in Great Britain in 2016 by
Biteback Publishing Ltd
Westminster Tower
3 Albert Embankment
London SE1 7SP
Copyright © Paul Cleary 2016
Also published by Black Inc., an imprint of Schwartz Publishing Pty Ltd, in 2016

ISBN 978-1-78590-100-3

10 9 8 7 6 5 4 3 2 1

A CIP catalogue record for this book is available from the British Library.

Text design and typesetting by Tristan Main

Map page x: A map showing the location of the Norwegian Sea in the North Atlantic Ocean. Created by Norman Einstein, 25 August 2005.

Printed and bound in Great Britain by
CPI Group (UK) Ltd, Croydon CR0 4YY

CONTENTS

CHRONOLOGY

1905   Norway becomes an independent nation, ending a 90-year union with Sweden and 400 years of foreign control.

1909   After three years of political turmoil, parliament passes the final version of the 'concession law', which ensures that Norway's natural resources, principally hydro, would revert to the state when developed by foreign investors.

1940   Nazi Germany invades; a formidable Norwegian resistance army emerges.

1945   US President Truman claims sovereign rights to the US Continental Shelf.

1958   Convention on the Continental Shelf is agreed.

1962   Phillips Petroleum seeks exclusive rights to the Norwegian Continental Shelf.

1963   Norway claims sole rights over its un-delimited continental shelf.

1964   Convention on the Continental Shelf enters into force.

1965   Norway concludes North Sea maritime boundary agreements, based on the principle of the median line, and licenses first blocks.

1969   Phillips finds the super-giant Ekofisk field; Norway declares it will take a direct equity share in fields awarded from this year.

1971   Ekofisk commences production; industry committee report outlines ten key 'commandments' for state-directed development of oil resources.

1972   Tripartite regulatory regime introduced, which becomes known internationally as 'the Norwegian model'.

1974   Mobil discovers the super-giant Statfjord field; Norwegian government shocks industry with plan for a super-profit tax of 40 per cent, on top of 50 per cent corporate tax rate; companies threaten to leave Norway.

1977   *Bravo* platform of Ekofisk facility spills 120,000 barrels of oil.

1979   The super-giant field known as Troll is discovered by Shell; Statfjord begins production but Norway is heavily indebted after investing in the project.

1980   Collapse of an Ekofisk platform kills 123 people.

1981   Parliament approves the 894 kilometre Statpipe to cross the 300-metre-deep Norwegian trench and bring Statfjord gas onshore.

1985   Statpipe and processing facility completed, becoming the catalyst for large-scale onshore development of petrochemical industry.

1990   Parliament creates the Government Petroleum Fund.

1992   Norway floats its exchange rate.

1995   Troll field begins production.

1996   Government makes first deposit into new petroleum fund.

1998   Central bank's fund managers begin investing in equities in 21 countries.

2001   UN human development report ranks Norway as having the highest socio-economic standard of living in the world, a position held every year since then.

2004   Norway's oil and gas production peaks; ethical investment guidelines introduced.

2006   Fund name changed to Government Pension Fund Global.

2007   Share of equity investments in the fund increased from 40 to 60 per cent.

2008   The fund is authorised to invest in real estate.

2015   After increasing sevenfold in the decade to 2015, the fund peaks at just over US$900 billion amid volatility on global markets.

2016   The government's projections indicate that, based on the current dollar-krone exchange rate, the fund is projected to exceed US$1 trillion in January 2020.

MAP OF NORWAY AND ITS MARITIME TERRITORY

PROLOGUE

ON A WINTRY DAY IN LATE NOVEMBER 1974, EXECUTIVES FROM the world's most powerful oil companies filed into a grand quadrangular building in Oslo. Adorned with a white wedding cake façade, Victoria Terrasse had served as the headquarters for the Nazi security police during the Second World War. Now it was the head office for the Ministry of Foreign Affairs, and the government had chosen this venue because it was about to assert its sovereignty like never before. Most of the executives assembled in the large auditorium came from the big American companies. They operated in the four corners of the world, where they were accustomed to deciding how they'd do business. But Norway, which at the time had a population of just 3.85 million people, knew it needed to take control of its destiny and reap a much larger share of the benefits from the once-only extraction of its petroleum wealth.

A year earlier, Arab oil producers had formed the cartel known as the Organization of Petroleum Exporting Countries (OPEC), which slashed production and triggered a quadrupling of oil prices, thus ending a halcyon era of abundant fossil fuel. The following year, oil companies reported spectacular increases in profit. Norway's economic advisers quickly realised the tax regime that had been put in place a few years back wasn't designed for this new era of rising prices, and would deny the country tens of billions of dollars of revenue. Foreign companies exploring in Norway's part of the North Sea had discovered two mammoth oilfields over the past five years, and several smaller ones as well. Firm and wise stewardship of this endowment was called for.

In the five years since oil was discovered in 1969, Norway had learned a great deal about the powerful oil industry and it was now ready to extract the maximum possible share of revenue. It had set up a national oil company and given it a mission to generate direct ownership and profits for the state, and to drive the involvement of locals in the development of the industry. It had created a policy that allowed the state to take a direct equity stake in oilfields should they prove to be very profitable, without having to invest in the exploration costs. It was what might be known as a cake-and-eat-it policy. But on the revenue front, the existing tax regime still meant that any super profits would be collected by the companies, not the government of Norway.

Norway had the benefit of a very capable public service that had a long tradition of dealing with powerful foreign interests, most notably the companies that developed Norway's hydro resources in the early 1900s. The officials convinced the Labour government to move quickly and decisively to grab what they knew was rightfully theirs. Finance ministry officials were able to draw on a network of Norwegian executives who had been seconded to work inside foreign oil companies. Ostensibly, this was part of a plan to train Norway's inexperienced engineers, but the network proved to be a veritable fifth column that could supply the government with valuable information about these multinationals. The informants told the officials just how far they could push Big Oil. According to the economic historian Einar Lie, their aim was simple: to squeeze every last drop of excess profit while ensuring that the foreign oil rigs remained in operation.[1]

*

Not long after the executives had settled into their seats, finance officials explained that companies would now pay a special tax of 40 per cent on top of Norway's already high corporate tax rate of 50 per cent. The executives added the two figures together and thought they could be paying up to 90 per cent – at least, that was what the oil executives said when they breathlessly briefed the media after the meeting.[2] Norway's audacious move was described by the executives as being 'far more onerous' than what was being proposed by the UK government.[3] In fact, this surprise revenue grab encouraged the UK's treasury to be equally brave; at the time it was toying with the idea of an additional profits tax but had been reluctant to give details.[4]

Even more audacious than the rate of the special tax was its design. The proposed regime, which would see the government determining selling prices and the cost base for projects, was designed to drive a stake through the heart of tax minimisation by these global corporations.

Despite Norway's boldness, Big Oil kept its rigs in Norway's part of the North Sea, known as the Norwegian Continental Shelf (NCS), because the region remained an attractive place to invest and because it could gain no support from Norway's conservative party. Even though conservatives are traditionally great advocates of lower taxes, Norway's conservatives agreed with the higher rate and refrained from political opportunism. This is remarkably different to what has transpired in many other countries, where oil companies have been able to win support by dividing and conquering the political class. Even to this day, both sides of Norwegian politics remain firmly in favour of the tax regime.[5] Unlike other resource-rich countries, Norway was showing how to become the master rather than the servant of resource multinationals. That November 1974 meeting was a decisive step along the way towards reaping the maximum national benefit from the country's resource wealth.

*

Walk around the main streets of Oslo today, and what you'll see is surprisingly modest. Norway is distinctly lacking in grand edifices or other trophies that attest to its triumph as a petroleum producer. One of the very few such monuments is the sleek, iceberg-inspired Opera House overlooking Oslo Fjord, but that was finished ahead of schedule in 2008 and came in under its reasonable budget of $500 million. The main shopping centres are still old-style high streets, rather than modern-day mega-malls. Most government offices blend into the low-rise streetscapes and there is an absence of expensive vehicles on the road (other than a growing fleet of electric vehicles that run on the country's abundant hydro-electric power). Even Apple, which has planted its grandiose glass-fronted showrooms around the world, operates out of small shopfronts in the Norwegian capital.

As a society, Norwegians have remained true to the sentiment put to visiting oil executives in the late 1960s of wanting to eschew the euphoria of oil riches. This record is all the more remarkable because many other countries, and not just poor ones, have blown their boom-time windfalls on largesse, whether in the form of grand edifices, military hardware, white elephant projects or cash splashes for swinging voters.

Norway's experience is particularly instructive because of a misperception found in much academic literature and media commentary about the effect on countries of plentiful natural resources. This misperception is exemplified by Michael Ross in *The Oil Curse*: 'Petroleum wealth is overwhelmingly a problem for low- and middle-income countries, not rich, industrialised ones.'[6] Yet the view that resource-rich developed countries – such as Australia, Canada, the United States and the United Kingdom – have all astutely managed their resources is a flawed one. It's true that they may not be run by authoritarian regimes, but these countries can't be said to have exercised good governance and long-term strategy over the development of their non-renewable resources. At the end of the UK's first decade as an oil-rich nation, for example, the country had to ask the International Monetary Fund for a $4 billion bail-out, which is still the biggest facility ever extended by the emergency lender.[7]

Norway is alone in the developed world in having successfully kept most of the windfall from its oil and gas wealth – 90 per cent of cash flow now accrues to the Norwegian state.[8] And only Norway has set up sound institutions to manage this boom-time bonus for generations to come. At the start of its oil era, Norway was a middle-income country with a per capita GDP just ahead of Greece, and by the end of the 1970s it was heavily indebted to the rest of the world. Its net foreign liabilities as a share of GDP peaked at 40 per cent. But its effective taxation and disciplined savings strategy have since turned it from a net debtor into one of the world's biggest creditors. Its net foreign assets are worth 185 per cent of GDP, or around $760 billion, and they've risen even more sharply when converted back into local currency as a result of Norway's flexible exchange rate (one advantage of not being part of the euro). During a twenty-year period of relatively high oil prices, Norway salted away $870 billion in a long-term sovereign wealth fund. Despite lower oil prices, the fund is still growing and is on track to hit $1 trillion in 2020.

When compared with Canada and Australia, two industrialised nations with Westminster political institutions and substantial resource sectors, Norway's achievement is absolutely monumental.

Canada, with a comparable energy and mineral sector that generates 14 per cent of GDP, has established just one small sovereign wealth fund.[9] The oil-rich state of Alberta showed some foresight when it set up a future fund in 1976 to save windfall revenue, but it was repeatedly plundered by politicians, and the lack of good governance is evident today in its balance of C$18 billion ($13 billion).[10] Australia, with a rapidly growing mineral and energy sector, has performed no better. Even after its biggest resources boom, Australia has failed to build up rainy-day assets and its net foreign debt has hit the trillion-dollar mark in local currency. When the boom began in the early 2000s, Australia's foreign liabilities stood at around $A400 billion ($305 billion). By March 2016, they had more than doubled to A$1012 billion ($750 billion), or around 60 per cent of GDP.[11] Australia does have a sovereign wealth fund, the Future Fund, but its assets of around A$120 billion ($87 billion) are expressly linked to future pensions for public servants.

Norway offers the best example in the world today of how to govern extraction of non-renewable resources, but it is by no means perfect. The country made mistakes in the early years by allowing development to run ahead of safety, leading to the loss of many young lives in the 1970s and 1980s. The focus on onshore development involved high risks that pushed the technological frontier and led to massive cost blow-outs. The country is now licensing new development in the Arctic region, which is questionable on both technical and moral grounds. Norway can also be criticised for relying too heavily on oil production, which has meant that about one-quarter of its national income has been directly or indirectly tied to a single commodity.

But there's a great deal that can be learned from the Norwegian experience. Its long-term strategy and firm management, which, as this book explains, has its origins as far back as the early 1900s, is salutary reading for resource-rich countries as they grapple with the aftermath of the biggest mineral and energy boom and bust since the early 1970s. Norway is the small country that's become the big exception to the resource curse thesis. Its consensus-based political system allowed it to make far-reaching decisions from the very beginning, in stark contrast to other resource-rich countries.

OUT OF THE DARKNESS

'I was born dying.'
    Norway's greatest artist, Edvard Munch, on the poverty and
    despair that prevailed during his upbringing in working-class
                                                    Oslo, late 1800s

WHEN THE WORLD-FAMOUS ECONOMIST AND DEMOGRAPHER Thomas Malthus visited cold and remote Norway in the late 1790s, he observed a Danish-controlled territory that was living on the very margin of human existence. Not only did the sun shine for just a few hours per day during winter, and not at all in the far north, Norway's 875,000 people survived on what they could grow in small plots or catch in rivers and the sea.[12] But Malthus also saw that while these descendants of Vikings were no longer plundering foreign shores, they were still very much dependent on the sea as the country possessed very little arable land. People had to live within severe climatic and financial constraints, and young people often deferred marriage and starting a family in order to get ahead.[13]

Things got a whole lot worse not long after Malthus's visit. The Napoleonic wars led to North Sea naval blockades in the early part of the 1800s, which precipitated economic collapse and widespread hunger. One result of these wars was Denmark's transfer of Norway to Sweden. After a brief war with Sweden in 1814, Norway agreed to accept a union with its big neighbour despite having created its own parliament and constitution. Towards the latter part of that century, rapid population growth proved unsustainable as crop failures led to more famine, culminating in the mass exodus of more than 1 million Norwegians, most of whom found their way to the United States.[14] It was desperation and emigration on a similar scale to the Irish famine.

In the nineteenth century Norway diversified its very basic economy by drawing on centuries of experience gained from seafaring ancestors. The country became the base for global shipping fleets, and by the early twentieth century about 10 per cent of global tonnage was registered in Norway. Some estimates put the Norwegian registered fleet as the third-largest fleet in the world at the time, and one that generated a major source of foreign currency.[15] Ports and towns along the west coast became service centres for this new industry. While a wealthy elite rose as a result, life remained a struggle for many ordinary Norwegians, even for those living in the capital, then known as Christiana. The life of renowned artist Edvard Munch attests to this experience. Munch's most famous work, *The Scream*, a portrait of a ghostly figure overcome with anguish and grief, isn't a creation from the psychedelic '60s as some might think. This evocative image reflected Munch's own harrowing upbringing in impoverished tenement housing in Christiana during the late 1800s. Munch lost two siblings and his mother to illnesses that ravaged the population at the time. These tragic deaths put his father on a path of religious fundamentalism, and left the young Edvard a deeply traumatised individual. 'I was born dying,' he said as an old man. 'Sickness, insanity and death were the dark angels standing guard at my cradle and they have followed me throughout my life.'[16]

It was not until 1905 that Norway finally emerged as a fully independent country, following 400 years of Danish or Swedish control. At the time of gaining independence, Norway was faced with strong interest from foreign investors, most notably France and Germany, who wanted to build dams to produce hydro-electric power. This issue triggered intense debate in the country and led to the fall of two governments. The conflict was finally resolved when the new parliament passed the *Concession Act 1909*, which ensured that these resources remained in state hands.[17] The country might have been small but it had developed a capable public service, which took a firm and principled approach to securing the best deal for the new nation.

This brief period of growth and prosperity ended abruptly in 1940 when Norway was drawn into the Second World War. Its location on the north-eastern edge of the North Sea, and its 20,000 kilometre coastline, made it the perfect place for the Nazis to exercise control over this strategic maritime area. German paratroopers invaded Norway on 9 April 1940, and by 5 May all resistance in the south ceased, forcing the king and the government to take flight for England. Under the Nazis, a new government was led by Vidkun Quisling, whose name became synonymous with enemy collaboration.

While the typically tall and fair-haired Norwegians might have been perfect candidates for Hitler's Aryan master race, a formidable movement of civil disobedience and armed resistance emerged over the next five years. By the end of the war, a resistance army of 40,000 men and women, known as Milorg, had formed, and it proved decisive at pivotal moments in the war. This resistance produced many legendary figures on the ground, but the primary mastermind was a young lawyer named Jens Christian Hauge, who assumed control of Milorg at the age of just twenty-eight. Hauge, whose slight build and dark hair made him look untypically Norwegian, had been a law lecturer and mid-level bureaucrat when he joined Milorg in December 1941. By the end of 1942, he was chief of military staff and a member of the Military Council, the highest decision-making body in the resistance. According to an account by resistance fighter Tore Gjelsvik,

Hauge's 'authority and efficiency made him the most influential leader of Milorg for the rest of the war'.[18]

At first, Hauge faced the challenge of presiding over an army with few weapons, but once the British began supplying his forces from the air, he had to restrain the blood lust of both radical and exuberant members of his growing army. As Gunnar Sønsteby, the most highly decorated member of Milorg, once said: 'When your country is taken over by 100,000 Germans, you get angry.'[19] Hauge reasoned that a great deal of his troops' desired actions would be futile in military terms, while the payback by the Germans on ordinary Norwegians would be savage. When two Gestapo officers were killed in April 1942 in Tælavåg, the Germans retaliated by destroying the town and killing thirty-one people. So Hauge outlined a policy of moderation to make Milorg a more disciplined and effective operation. 'To activate the campaign by attacks on the enemy at the present juncture would be a fatal mistake,' he wrote in operational guidelines drafted in 1943.[20] Hauge was a meticulous planner. He developed a card system that was used to protect operatives in the event that one of their contacts was captured. The system showed clearly who worked with whom. Those who had been working with captured operatives would be moved to safety.

Three defining actions of Norwegian forces in this war showed the value of this disciplined strategy. The first involved a team of nine Norwegians who in February 1943 scaled a 100 metre precipice and blew up the stock of heavy water that was destined for Germany's atomic bomb program.[21] These amateur warriors succeeded where a team of thirty British Royal Engineers had failed a few months earlier. The Germans recovered from this setback and succeeded in producing more heavy water, but they still had to ship it out of the country. Norway's resistance network was so well organised that it was able to destroy the consignment of heavy water supplies en route to Germany. Milorg's finest hour arrived in December 1944, when it carried out as many as thirty coordinated acts of sabotage aimed at stemming Germany's redeployment of forces to the Ardennes during the Battle of the Bulge.

A mastermind in war and peace. Jens Christian Hauge, dressed in a suit, with Norwegian defence chiefs and future US president Dwight D. Eisenhower, in his role as Supreme Allied Commander of NATO in 1951. The group is watching a flyover of Thunder jet fighters at Oslo airfield. Image courtesy of Scanpix.

Hauge was rightly recognised as a hero after the war, and he stood on the podium next to the king during the victory parade in Oslo. He was appointed defence minister in the Labour government that presided over the country's postwar development. The war had a profound effect on the national psyche of Norway; the country became more outward looking, and it sought to engage with the new institutions that were emerging in the postwar era. Norway funded the building of the United Nations Security Council

Chamber. It is adorned with a mural that carries the motifs of anchors, wheat and hearts on a blue damask background symbolising faith, hope and charity. The first secretary-general of the UN was the former Norwegian foreign minister Trygve Lie, who had served in the government-in-exile during the war.

Hauge used the authority and efficiency he had exercised over Milorg to play a key role in making Norway more engaged in defence and foreign affairs. He became the architect of Norway's integration into the Western defence alliance. In 1949, Norway formally joined the fledgling North Atlantic Treaty Organization (NATO), thus ending the country's previous policy of neutrality and isolation. As Norway shared a border with the Soviet Union, Hauge pushed for a rapid expansion of defence spending, despite strong opposition. His war experience made him staunchly pro-American and pro-nuclear, and it was revealed decades after the war that his name appeared in the files of the Office of Strategic Services, the forerunner of the Central Intelligence Agency between 1942 and 1945. While this probably meant that the CIA had unilaterally claimed Hauge as someone who could be relied on to help America, it was also consistent with his positive views towards the Americans.

In the decades immediately after the war, Labour governments developed their own brand of social democracy based on strong labour rights, extensive social welfare benefits and industrialisation. The notion of postponing immediate consumption in order to save and invest for the future was at the heart of the strategy outlined by the Labour Party, which ruled the country for the first eighteen years of the postwar era. Einar Gerhardsen, prime minister for fourteen of those years, explained later that the community accepted Norway's high rates of investment in order to lift living standards. He said: 'In 1945 it was clear for everyone that the "cake" was too small. If living standards were to rise, the "cake" had to grow. This meant that production had to grow to lay the basis for an increasing affluence.'²² And indeed this is what the country did for a sustained period after the war, as it achieved the highest rate of investment of any OECD country. Gross fixed capital investment peaked at 32 per cent of GDP in 1958.²³ These high rates of investment mainly reflected the country's focus on hydro-electric generation and the energy-intensive industries that coalesced around this cheap source of power. All of this heavy industry was very capital intensive, making the country dependent on foreign capital. Despite the cost to immediate consumption, the government managed to achieve strong support for this strategy. Economist Petter Nore, who worked in the petroleum ministry for a decade, says postwar Norway was characterised by a high degree of social consensus with very low rates of industrial action. In his PhD thesis about the first decade of Norway's oil development, Nore wrote: 'One of the reasons why the Norwegian population was prepared to accept high investment rates and corresponding cuts in their immediate standard of living in the postwar period was the high degree of legitimacy that the Norwegian government enjoyed.'²⁴

While the Labour Party steered a steady course, Jens Christian Hauge experienced mixed fortunes following his spectacular rise during and after the war. By the time he was forty, he had been forced out of his defence role because he clashed with the army generals and the parliament. The meticulous approach he brought to running a guerrilla army didn't seem to work in peacetime. Hauge angered his cabinet colleagues when he used funds allocated for domestic consumption and homebuilding for a rapid expansion of defence capability. He achieved his goal two years ahead of schedule in 1952, when he stepped down as minister.²⁵ He had also advocated strongly in favour of building up Norway's nuclear capacity, diverting funds away from an expansion of conventional weapons to this end. After a short stint as justice minister in 1955, his political career was over. At this time, however, he had a large young family and was happy to return to practising law while remaining an influential figure in the Labour Party.

But Hauge again rose to prominence in the early 1970s when Norway had to mobilise the country to deal with another foreign challenge, this time the influx of powerful multinationals following the discovery of oil. Hauge emerged as an influential industrial strategist, albeit in an unofficial capacity. The lessons of the war came to the fore in the way that Norway faced this new challenge. Instead of unleashing an oil boom, Norway adopted a policy of controlled development and moderation so that the country could develop private-sector capacity and government institutions to benefit fully from its new-found wealth. As Hauge and his team of confidants saw it, Norway needed to do much more than produce another commodity – the oil should be used to help the country to industrialise and generate lasting returns. This was the genesis of a strategy that would handsomely reward Norway for decades to come.

2

INTO THE DEEP

'The Viking came out in them. They were quite ruthless.'
Former British civil servant on North Sea
negotiations with Norway

MOST PEOPLE HAVE SEEN THE GRAINY BLACK AND WHITE footage of the lunar landing in 1969, and some may even remember the September 1962 speech by President John F. Kennedy in which he declared that by the end of the decade the United States would land a man on the moon. But few people know anything of President Harry S. Truman's proclamation a generation earlier, even though it fired the starting gun on an equally challenging type of exploration of a new frontier. Just six weeks after Japan ended the Second World War by surrendering in August 1945, Truman laid claim to the resources underneath the seabed extending from the coastline of the US. The Truman Proclamation, as it became known, would trigger human and technological effort on a scale comparable to the quest to reach the moon, but instead of reaching for the skies, Truman's proclamation would marshal immense resources to brave the high seas and drill deep into the seabed.

The Truman Proclamation was squarely aimed at petroleum, and it anticipated the development of new technology that could be used to access these offshore resources.[26] 'With modern technological progress their utilization is already practicable or will become so at an early date,' Truman noted. But even Truman had no idea of the scale of technological development that would result from this proclamation, especially once oil became a more valuable commodity. Over the next three to four decades, oil companies would sink wells 3000–4000 metres deep into the seabed to explore for oil, and they would build structures taller than the world's tallest skyscrapers to extract these resources when proven commercially viable. It wouldn't be an engineering solution exclusively, as this industry would rely heavily on incredible feats of courage and daring from men sent hundreds of metres below sea level, often for weeks at a time, to build pipelines and keep the oil rigs in good shape while breathing an artificial mixture of helium and oxygen. Nor could Truman have imagined that the place where this ingenuity and daring would be pushed to the limit wasn't off the coast of the US, but in the wild and icy waters off the west coast of Norway.

American companies had been extracting oil off the beach at Summerland, California, from 1897 onwards, and in 1938 the first offshore oil rig was built in the Gulf of Mexico, though it was wiped out by a hurricane two years later.[27] But until 1945, countries had not looked far beyond their coastline for undersea resources. Most remained limited to the territorial sea, which was defined by the distance of long-range cannons – twelve nautical miles. Truman proclaimed that exercising jurisdiction over resources beneath the high seas was 'reasonable and just' because the continental shelf may be regarded as an extension of the land mass under the sea. This seabed would have been part of the continent when sea levels were lower, and in some instances it can extend for hundreds of nautical miles. Significantly, the proclamation made clear that as the US was laying claim to the contiguous continental shelf that extended from its land mass, it would reach agreements with neighbouring states that might also claim the same continental shelf, and it would negotiate these agreements in an 'equitable' manner. Thus, the proclamation became the template for later international moves to codify how neighbouring states should settle their competing claims.

At the time of the proclamation, remote and isolated Norway was still recovering from five years of Nazi occupation and repression, but it was this country, arguably more than any other, that rose to Truman's challenge and embarked on a new North Sea adventure with considerable gusto, culminating in the first major discovery of oil in 1969, just two months after the lunar landing.

Norway's North Sea oil boom didn't happen right away, because it took some time for the far-reaching implications of the Truman Proclamation to impact both on law-making within the US and on international conventions presided over by the newly formed United Nations. It wasn't until 1953 that the US parliament passed the *Outer Continental Lands Act*, which specified how the government would allocate rights to resources beneath its continental shelf. This unilateral initiative sparked a global push to codify rights relating to the high seas and was followed by the 1958 United Nations Conference on the Law of the Sea, which ran from 24 February to 27 April that year and was attended by eighty-six countries. The conference was well attended because coastal states had an interest in ensuring that they were represented. It led to the first Convention on the Continental Shelf, which allowed states to exercise sovereign rights of exploration and exploitation over their continental shelf to a depth of 200 metres. Article 2 of the convention states that: 'The coastal State exercises over the continental shelf rights for the purpose of exploring it and exploiting its natural resources.'[28]

Like the Truman Proclamation, the convention set out a principle for resolving the competing claims of adjacent states, stating that a 50–50 split, or the median line, should be used in the absence of a specific agreement. The convention didn't have any immediate practical effect because it required twenty-two countries to ratify it before it could 'enter into force'. Norway was in no rush to do so because the government was convinced that fossil fuel resources were unlikely to be found beneath the seabed extending off the country's coast. In a February 1958 memo to the Ministry of Foreign Affairs, Norway's Geological Survey had, based on the rudimentary analysis that had been conducted at the time, largely dismissed any such prospect. 'The chances of finding coal, oil or sulphur on the continental shelf off the Norwegian coast can be discounted,' the survey agency had written in February that year ahead of the continental shelf conference in Geneva.

But the following year the giant Groningen gas field was discovered in Holland, and while it was located onshore, seismic surveys showed that the gas-bearing structures extended far underneath the seabed of the North Sea. It proved to be one of the biggest gas fields ever discovered and remains in production today.[29] The discovery of a potential new source of hydrocarbons, located very close to European markets, sparked the interest of the big oil companies, which had become concerned about supply from the Middle East. According to Shell: 'Interest in the North Sea as a prospective zone of exploration became marked in the late 1950s after the first Suez crisis of 1956–57.'[30] So the initial interest began with a political event that threatened supply, and the Groningen discovery merely showed the oil companies where to look. Shell sought exploration rights from the UK government in 1959, and within three years, Shell, BP and Esso began a joint seismic survey off the UK and Dutch coast. These three companies were among the seven global oil giants, also known as the 'seven sisters'.[31] Interest in Norway came not from the big companies but the middle-ranked Phillips Petroleum, which first made contact with the Norwegian government via its embassy in Bonn, West Germany, in 1962. Phillips sought open-ended rights to explore and develop potential petroleum resources. The Phillips interest came about after a senior executive took a vacation in Europe and noticed the oil rigs around the Groningen field.[32]

Some popular accounts of these events claim that Phillips wanted a total monopoly over Norway's maritime area, but it was more a case of the company seeking to secure a central position, which was similar to what Shell had achieved in neighbouring Denmark.[33] Even so, the company made an offer of upfront cash, US$162,000 per month, to secure these rights.[34] A Phillips delegation then met in October 1962 with Trygve Lie, the former UN secretary-general who now chaired a committee responsible for securing foreign investment to Norway. In a country that was short of foreign capital, Lie was known as Norway's 'dollar ambassador', but he gave no commitment to the Phillips executives. There was no need for the Norwegian government to make a hasty decision, because at this time two other groups were also seeking exploration rights. They were the Shell-led consortium and another that involved two French companies. Lie referred the matter to the Ministry of Foreign Affairs, which in turn assigned the task to one of its brightest, the 45-year-old lawyer Jens Evensen. Evensen's advice led Norway to finally issue a royal decree on 31 May 1963 that laid claim to the seabed and the resources on its continental shelf. Significantly, the country seized on the right to a median line in the UN convention. The decree stated:

> The sea-bed and the subsoil in the submarine areas outside the coast of the Kingdom of Norway are under Norwegian sovereignty as regards exploitation and exploration of natural resources, as far as the depth of the superjacent waters admits of exploitation of natural resources, within as well as outside the maritime boundaries otherwise applicable, but not beyond the median line in relation to other states.[35]

This was a far-sighted move on the part of Evensen, because even a decade after the decree was issued, other countries were still settling agreements that did not follow the median-line principle, most notably Indonesia and Australia (which in turn culminated in Indonesia's bloody invasion of the Portuguese colony of East Timor and twenty-four years of brutal occupation). The decree stood Norway in good stead for securing a fair division of the North Sea's potential resources. Like the US, Norway was staking out its claim to the seabed even before the new convention came into effect. Two months later, Norway awarded the right to conduct seismic surveys – as distinct from exploration rights – to the three groups: Shell, BP and Esso; France's BRP; and Phillips.[36]

A FEW GOOD MEN

At this pivotal moment in its history, Norway knew next to nothing about how the complex oil industry worked, and it had to negotiate with much bigger countries and powerful multinationals that were adept at exploiting inexperienced countries. It was clearly getting itself into a David and Goliath struggle. But the country did have at its disposal a number of key politicians who were determined to fight for their country's best interests, and they were advised by a small but very capable public service.

Jens Evensen was one of a handful of men who played a key role in formulating policy to best serve the country's interests. The son of a sausage maker from working-class Oslo, he became a barrister and gained a PhD from Harvard. He headed the legal department within the Ministry of Foreign Affairs and chaired a committee responsible for Norway's continental shelf.[37] Evensen came from the generation whose formative years coincided with the political, social and economic upheaval that followed the Great Depression, and lasted through the 1930s. This process allowed long-standing class conflict to be resolved, and it led to a more cohesive society. After drafting Norway's claim over the seabed resources on its continental shelf, Evensen then had to deal with an aggressive plan by Britain to fast-track negotiations over the seabed in the North Sea.

Evensen rose to the fore in early 1964 when the United Kingdom was preparing to commence maritime boundary negotiations to divide up the North Sea and launch its own oil boom. In February 1964, the UK embassy in Oslo sent an aide-mémoire to the government of Norway outlining its position on the North Sea. Even before negotiations had begun, the UK offered favourable terms to Norway and other countries with overlapping claims in the North Sea. Seven countries had claims and, notwithstanding the median-line principle in the convention, maritime law was still in its infancy and it remained to be seen how they would be resolved. It was possible that natural features such as trenches could be used to delineate the seabed. In the case of Norway's area, the seabed was defined by a deep trench located close to Norway's southern and western coasts. As the North Sea is relatively shallow, with average depths of around 60 metres, the Norwegian Trench is a marked feature, plumbing depths of 350 metres off the west coast of Norway and reaching 700 metres near the southern coast.

The British government outlined in the mémoire how it was planning to open up the North Sea for exploration by oil companies following passage of the Continental Shelf Bill. The UK government would 'propose that the dividing line should be calculated on median line principles', which greatly favoured Norway.[38] The communiqué then spelled out how islands might be included in mapping the coastline, which again favoured Norway because of its long and jagged coastline. Upon receiving the document, Jens Evensen, who had anticipated that the trench would come into play, could not believe that the UK government was offering such favourable terms. He urged the Oslo government to promptly work towards an agreement, writing in the margin of the mémoire: 'We must strike immediately because of difficulties with the Norwegian trench.' While the offer of the median line by the UK government might seem exceedingly fair, it was made in order to avoid getting bogged down in lengthy negotiations.

Britain's stance in the North Sea negotiations was really being driven by necessity. Postwar Britain was weighed down by a trade deficit and it desperately needed a new source of foreign income. A big part of the country's financial woes were attributed to oil imports. But there were deeper problems relating to Britain's anti-quated industrial structure, which was unable to modernise in the face of increased competition from the Continent. Even though the mid-1960s saw the height of Beatlemania, and England defeating Germany in the World Cup, the UK's economic fortunes were declining under the Labour government led by Edward Heath.

Ahead of reaching boundary agreements, the UK government planned to issue exploration licences in areas 'which must indis-putably be regarded as falling within the United Kingdom sphere ... so that interested concerns may proceed with the exploi-tation of the natural resources of those areas'. In May 1965 the UK embarked on its first licensing round, offering 348 blocks, each of them covering an area of 250 square kilometres. On the eve of the commencement of negotiations, Britain's financial press declared that the country would 'negotiate mightily for its every last corner' of the North Sea,[39] but in fact the foreign affairs department wanted a speedy resolution with Norway in order to facilitate development. As part of this strategy, Britain ratified the Conven-tion on the Continental Shelf in June 1964, the twenty-second country to do so, thus bringing it into force. In the same month Norway's parliament passed a new law governing submarine natu-ral resources, which was to provide the basis for all subsequent petroleum legislation. Norway, however, saw no need to ratify the convention and instead focused on reaching a settlement with the UK and Denmark. The country in fact never ratified the 1958 convention because there was 'no pressing need' to do so.[40]

In March 1965, after less than a year of negotiations, the UK and Norway reached an agreement to divide the North Sea. In international treaty terms, this was a remarkably quick resolution, especially given the fact that once ratified, such boundaries cannot be changed. Despite the way the UK media had raised expectations about Britain's negotiating stance, the agreement generated very little tension between the two countries, and scant public interest and publicity. As foreshadowed in the aide-mémoire, not only did Britain not seek to exploit the trench, it also agreed to include outlying islands and skerries, which had the effect of pushing the boundary even further away from the Norwegian coastline. The end result was a Norwegian maritime area that was as large as Norway's land surface.[41]

With the boundary in place, Norway joined the rush to license exploration rights. In April 1965, just one month after signing the agreement with Britain, Evensen advised the Norwegian government to open up a massive area in the southern part of the North Sea for exploration. Evensen reasoned that it was to Norway's advantage that they bring in foreign oil companies to explore and find out more about the extent of the country's potential oil wealth. Norway was competing against Britain and other North Sea nations that were rushing to offer exploration licences, and it risked being left behind. Evensen's judgment was backed by *The Economist* magazine, which said the country faced stiff competition from the UK and Holland: 'The Norwegian concessions appear to have been granted in the nick of time.'[42] The first concession round saw Norway take a big risk by awarding a total of seventy-eight blocks covering an area of 48,000 square kilometres, or 20 per cent of the Norwegian Continental Shelf. While this was half the area awarded by the UK in its first round, it covered nearly the whole area south of the 60th parallel.

Jens Evensen (left) with the minister of industry, Karl Trasti, looking at a map of the blocks to be offered in the first licensing round. Image courtesy of Scanpix.

Norway embarked on this endeavour even though it had very little oil industry expertise and understanding. Evensen was so lacking in technical experts that he asked for assistance from the local representative of Esso to help draft the fiscal package that was to underpin development, which clearly gave the oil companies an advantage. At the time of the round, a small office was emerging within the Ministry of Industry to deal with oil issues, but for the first few years it consisted of just three people. The very first employee in this new department, in late 1964, was the law graduate Nils B. Gulnes, who got the job because his boss heard from a neighbour that he spoke good English. Gulnes had previously served in the Royal Norwegian Navy. Early the following year he was joined by geologist Fredrik Hagemann and engineer Olav K. Christiansen, and then it was game on, as the country moved to license blocks just one month after securing the agreement with the UK. 'After that, everything happened fast. The legislation was in place by 9 April, and 278 blocks on the [Norwegian Continental Shelf] were put on offer four days later,' says Gulnes.[43] The small team worked closely with Evensen and did much of their work informally, with remarkably little committed to paper.[44] The team was free to develop a policy framework that has stood the test of time. The lack of debate in the parliament meant they were able to work for the first five years with little political interference.

At this time there was remarkably little interest among politicians about the potential of this new industry, largely because many people still thought that there was no oil to be found. When the first white paper on the oil industry went to parliament in 1965, it generated just thirty minutes of debate about the potential impact of seismic activity on fishing. 'Few people, if any, believed in the oil business,' says Gulnes. Hagemann, who came to the ministry from the Norwegian Geological Survey – the same organisation that in 1958 had dismissed any prospect of finding oil – said that few people believed Norway would find oil. 'Everyone else was pessimistic, including the politicians and industry,' he says.[45]

The position that Norway found itself in at the start of its oil era was not dissimilar to that faced by many resource-rich countries, especially those from the developing world that are faced with powerful corporate interests and competing nations, and an industry that is technically and legally complex. Despite concerns among oil executives that left-leaning Norway would seek tough terms, it unveiled an attractive package to the foreign companies. The initial royalty of 10 per cent was somewhat lower than the companies had been expecting, and in fact it was lower than the UK's 12.5 per cent royalty. Evensen had reasoned that as Norway was a small country and in competition with the UK and Holland, he had to make the terms competitive. He wanted the oil companies to commit to the country as much as possible and thereby increase the probability of finding out if Norway did in fact possess significant petroleum resources. One of Evensen's main concerns at the time was Norway's limited access to foreign currency, as the country lacked foreign investment.[46] Allowing the lawyers from foreign oil companies to help draft Norway's North Sea tax regime meant that the end result was indeed very competitive. Norway certainly began its entry into oil from a weak position, and as the Norwegian historian Helge Ryggvik has noted, the idea of a particularly radical oil policy 'can certainly not be ascribed to the very first chapter of Norway's oil history'.[47]

The design of this round dashed the hopes that mid-size oil company Phillips had held of playing a pivotal role in the country's oil development, but even so it was able to secure blocks with good prospects.[48] Norway's own companies had a very minor role; Norwegian businesses were represented with minor stakes in only twenty-one of the seventy-eight blocks. Over the next three years, Esso and Phillips found either dry or uncommercial wells, and interest in Norway's region of the North Sea began to wane, especially after the discovery of major fields on the British side.

IRAQI ANGEL

One morning in early 1968, 32-year-old Farouk Al-Kasim flew into Oslo's small airport with all of his belongings packed into a suitcase, and as he had several hours to wait for a train, he decided to introduce himself to the Ministry of Industry. Educated in petroleum geology at Imperial College London, where he had enrolled at the age of eighteen, Al-Kasim had worked for the British-administered Iraq Petroleum Company for more than a decade before deciding to relocate to Norway with his Norwegian wife, Solfrid, and their three children. Al-Kasim had wanted to ask the ministry for some contacts in Norway's nascent oil industry, but when he returned he found himself facing a panel who wanted to know everything about his education and experience in the oil industry. In fact, the panel consisted of Gulnes, Christiansen and Hagemann, Norway's entire oil administration at the time.[49]

Raised in the Iraqi port city of Basra amid flares from oil facilities that lit the night sky, Al-Kasim was one of five children, and he proved to be so promising at a young age that he started school in the second grade. His father was a disciplinarian school teacher who also ran an orphanage. Upon finishing school, he won a place in the first and only group of young Iraqis to be sent abroad by the Iraq Petroleum Company to study petroleum geology at Imperial College. In 1956, his final year, he was introduced to Solfrid by a mutual friend, and the two married later that year in South Ealing. The couple then headed to Iraq, where Al-Kasim worked in a well-paid role as one of the very first Iraqi executives to work for the Iraq Petroleum Company. He recalls the first time he walked into the exclusive club frequented by the British oil executives and their wives. He walked across to the bar, where he ordered a drink. When he turned to look around the room, he saw that all of the managers and their wives were staring at him. It was the first time they had seen an Iraqi enter the club who was not one of the waiters. Over the next decade the couple raised a family and led a very comfortable life, even though the military coup of 1967, which overthrew the royal family, meant having to contend with checkpoints and a heavy military presence in their daily lives.

Al-Kasim had left behind his comfortable life in Iraq because his youngest child had cerebral palsy and needed better medical care than was available in Iraq. Due to the military coup, getting the family out involved a smuggling operation. Solfrid took the two eldest on her passport for a purported holiday, while Al-Kasim used the excuse of medical treatment to take the youngest child out of the country.

Farouk Al-Kasim with Solfrid and their three children shortly after they arrived in Norway. Image courtesy of Al-Kasim family.

What struck Al-Kasim most about his adoptive country of Norway was that most of his colleagues and other people he met were quite fearful rather than excited about the prospect of discovering oil. Norwegians knew from the outset that oil could have disastrous consequences both for the economy and society as a whole. And when oil was discovered they became even more fearful. 'The country feared the social and economic consequences of an oil boom. The Groningen gas field had ruined the Dutch economy. Norway was aware of that; it had quite justified fears. And with the oil discovery Norwegians feared they'd be over-run by Texan oil workers who would be chewing gum, looking for girls and bringing prostitutes into the country,' he explains.[50]

The Royal Ministry of Industry was not nearly as grand as the name implies. At the time it was a small office of about thirty people with just a handful of technical advisers. While Al-Kasim's arrival was indeed timely, the ministry couldn't offer him a permanent job because he wasn't a Norwegian citizen, and in any case the salary would have been about one-third of what he had earned in Iraq. So they offered him a three-month contract to evaluate evidence from recent drilling operations and write a report. The job was short-term, but Al-Kasim was compensated with a very high salary, which was in fact higher than that of the prime minister.

Al-Kasim waded through a mountain of material that included seismic surveys and data from exploration programs. In 1967, Esso had found a small field that it named Balder, but it was then declared uncommercial. In 1968, Phillips drilled the thirteenth exploration well on Norway's side of the North Sea and found a field that became known as Cod, but Phillips dismissed its potential. Al-Kasim thought this latest find was 'a significant discovery'. While these apparently uncommercial wells were sapping interest among oil companies at the time, Al-Kasim realised that these recent finds were 'marginally interesting and could have been commercial'.[51] He was right. Phillips developed Cod in 1977 and produced 18 million barrels of oil, while Esso developed Balder thirty-two years later with reserves of 450 million barrels of oil. Al-Kasim noted that there were many 'very interesting structures' on the Norwegian Continental Shelf that most likely held mammoth oil and gas deposits. He concluded that 'in a very short time the oil companies would stumble on a super-giant'. After he handed in the report, the Norwegian ministry offered Al-Kasim a permanent position, making him one of the very first foreign nationals to be employed in the country's civil service. The government found a way to employ the person whom many Norwegians now regard as the country's most valuable immigrant.

3

COMMAND AND CONTROL

'*This is immoral!*'

William Martin, Phillips Petroleum vice president responding
to Jens Christian Hauge's demand for a 50 per cent share in
North Sea pipelines

THE NORTH SEA IS A FORMIDABLE PLACE MOST DAYS OF THE
year and it was no different in autumn 1969. A drilling rig contracted by the Oklahoma-based Phillips Petroleum was plying
these grim waters in what seemed like the vain search for black gold.
This operation showed how Norwegian companies had been quick to
move in on the potential opportunities; the drilling rig, the *Ocean
Viking*, has been built by Aker, one of Norway's oldest shipping companies. But so far, the *Viking* had not delivered. Phillips had already
drilled the thirty-second unsuccessful well on the Norwegian Continental Shelf and management was losing interest in devoting more
time and resources to what seemed to be a futile exercise. In mid-
1969, Phillips sought permission to abandon the program.[52] The
response from Norway's then embryonic petroleum authority was
firmly negative. It insisted that Phillips honour its contractual obligations and complete the agreed work program, or pay compensation.

Phillips relented mainly because it could not find any other
operator to take over its lease on the *Viking*.[53] It was also significant

that the Norwegians had designed their exploration programs based on the depth of drilling, not the amount of money spent. Norway's three-man petroleum administration had held a number of meetings with Britain's undersecretary for power, Angus Beckett, who told them how work programs specified in cash could be easily exhausted, giving companies the option of escaping their obligations. Beckett told the Norwegians that they should specify the number of wells down to certain depths. 'He gave us the most valuable advice,' says Gulnes, the lawyer working on oil issues for the Ministry of Industry.[54]

So Phillips continued a tradition of taking one last roll of the dice, just like when Colonel Drake found oil in Pennsylvania in 1859, and when oil was first discovered in Persia in 1908.[55] In late August, the workers on the rig began drilling Norway's thirty-third well, identified as 2/4-1, where they found gas at a depth of 1330 metres. They went down a further 300 metres where they encountered so much pressurised oil that they had to abandon the operation. 'Oil was gushing out of the borehole and it took a while to control it to the point that we eventually lost the well,' recalls the Italian geologist Max Melli, who was on board the *Viking*.[56] The well was plugged on 15 September. Four days later, company executives met with the Norwegian government officials and agreed to drill another well in a location about 1000 metres away from 2/4-1. Farouk Al-Kasim and his small team could see that Phillips had drilled into a 'gas chimney' that passed directly through the potential oil zone. 'We told them to move outside that chimney. That's exactly what they did,' he explains. The *Ocean Viking* began drilling a second well on 18 September. The drilling went on for thirty-eight days before reaching a depth of more than 3000 metres below the seabed, where a significant deposit of oil became apparent.[57] As the results had to be sent back to the UK for testing,[58] it was wasn't until 23 December that the Oslo government announced to the world that Norway had unearthed one of the biggest offshore discoveries ever made, one that is likely to remain in production until the middle of this century.

It's become part of Norwegian mythology that the find was made the day before Christmas, thereby adding a fairy-tale element to this history. Norwegians anecdotally believe this to be the case. The claim was repeated in a 2015 video made by the Norwegian government about the history of its oil development. But in fact the find was made in September, and then after evaluating the results, a senior executive at Phillips telephoned the minister of industry on 23 December and told him, 'I think we have an oilfield.'[59] To the Norwegians, the find proved that they had luck on their side. Had they not insisted that Phillips continue drilling, the company would no doubt have packed up and gone home, sending a clear signal to the rest of the industry that there was no oil to be found on Norway's side of the North Sea. Time and time again, Norwegians describe themselves as a lucky country, even though it was Norway's firm management that helped to make its luck.

The field was called Ekofisk by the drilling team, a made-up name that followed a pattern of naming each well with a successive letter of the alphabet and usually after a fish. As this was Phillips's fifth well, they were up to the letter 'e' at the time, but they couldn't think of a fish that started with the letter. 'Eel' was considered briefly but this didn't appeal, so the company put together the words 'echo' and 'fish' and came up with 'ekofisk' in Norwegian. Phillips had located a gigantic ten by five kilometre field 3000 metres below the seabed.[60] Ekofisk proved to be one of the world's biggest offshore oilfield, with 3.5 billion barrels of oil and 162 billion cubic metres of gas.[61]

The discovery of this oilfield says a lot about the entirely random nature of finding prehistoric accumulations of organic material in commercial quantities that have been 'cooked' for millions of years at just the right temperature, but it says a great deal more about the Norwegian way of running its oil business, even in this very early stage. First, Phillips could well have been drilling in British waters had Norway not secured a favourable maritime boundary with the United Kingdom. Ekofisk is almost equidistant between Norway and the UK and is tucked just inside the southeast corner of Norway's part of the continental shelf, along with several other major finds that followed. Second, the drilling operation was being closely monitored and managed by government officials who, while having very limited experience at this time, had their country's best interests at heart. Third, the discovery didn't lead to an oil rush as happened in neighbouring Holland and the UK, and numerous other resource-rich nations at this time. The response in Oslo was more of shock than awe, and the government subsequently took a moderate approach to development so that the nation could cautiously, methodically and astutely develop the policies, institutions and industrial capacity to deal with and fully benefit from the exploitation of Norway's new-found wealth.

While Norway seemed at this time an unlikely candidate to become a world leader in oil industry management, its public service had from the outset a strong tradition of focusing on the national interest, gained from more than half a century's experience in dealing with powerful corporate interests. This historical backdrop is crucial in understanding the elements behind Norway's three-way success as an oil producer, industrial champion and collector of the lion's share of the profit that flowed from its oil wealth. In the early part of the nineteenth century the country had been very much dependent on foreign capital; it did not have its own banking system until 1816 when the present-day central bank, Norges Bank, took on the role of the territory's first and only lender.[62] Prior to this time, Norwegian businesspeople had had to travel to neighbouring Sweden to secure loan capital. Norway had entered into a union with Sweden in 1814 under its own constitution after it was 'transferred' from Denmark, though it would not be fully independent until 1905 when this union was dissolved.[63]

When, in the early twentieth century, German and French interests wanted to develop the country's vast river systems to produce hydro-electric power, Norway's leaders adopted an approach that the Norwegian state, as owner of the resources, should seek to obtain what economists call the 'economic rent'. This term was coined by eighteenth-century British economist David Ricardo. While Ricardo is best known for his theory of comparative advantage, he also developed the concepts of surplus value, which could be defined in two ways. The first was profit, which he accepted as fair and reasonable, but a second type of surplus was called economic rent, generally obtained by monopolising control of fertile land, or other natural resources that were limited in supply. The landlords of feudal times, for example, became rich by controlling the most fertile land. Other classical economists such as Adam Smith were equally loathing of the aristocracy's ability to extract such unjust economic rent while at the same time creating immense inequality. In the case of Norway, however, its economic advisers looked for ways to control the economic rent for the benefit of the entire country.

This thinking was prominent when Norway granted concessions to foreign interests to develop its hydro resources.[64] Norway's concession law was strongly influenced by the progressive movement in the United States and the notable journalist and self-taught economist Henry George, who developed a radical interpretation of Ricardo's theory of economic rent in his 1879 book *Progress and Poverty*.[65] George argued that any surplus, or rent, accumulated as a result of developing natural resources should accrue to the public as a whole. In addition, the *Concession Act* included a key principle of returning the ownership of the hydro operations to the state after sixty years, without the payment of any compensation. Historian Helge Ryggvik writes: 'Norway had both a legal framework and a long political tradition of how to relate to large foreign companies seeking to exploit other countries' natural resources.'[66] Economist Petter Nore says the experience with the concession law became a perfect policy fit for dealing with the oil companies. He explains:

Norway was a poor country filled with natural resources when it became independent in 1905. There was then a rush of investment by international capital, a lot of it going into Norway's hydro-electric sector. Norway as a state needed to have rules to deal with this influx of big powerful companies, and it did this through the concession laws. Later, it came up with a broadly similar legal framework when the oil industry knocked on its door.[67]

By the time the foreign oil companies came to Norway in the mid-1960s, most of the hydro resources were in the hands of, or in the process of being transferred to, the government, and the country had learned an important lesson about the value of collecting economic rent and retaining state control of such assets.

This approach explains why Norway's 'few good men' began pushing from the outset for direct government interests in exploration concessions, which allowed the government to exercise rights in the event of a lucky strike. The industry department formally put this proposal to Jens Evensen in his capacity as chair of the newly formed National Petroleum Council (NPC) in 1968. (The NPC had been established in May that year as a high-level advisory body within the industry ministry on all oil-related issues, and was essentially a forerunner to a formal regulatory authority.) At first the idea seemed untenable because the area to be drilled was so vast. The NPC responded by saying that the Norwegian Continental Shelf was 'so extensive and so unexplored that such an undertaking on the part of the State would be highly hazardous … the investments would inevitably become so enormous that they would disrupt a

Norwegian State Budget'. But certainly the idea got people inside the government thinking, so that the NPC supported a modified proposal allowing the state to exercise its ownership right in the event of a big discovery. This change of heart followed a declaration by the Organization of the Petroleum Exporting Countries (OPEC) in the same year that its member countries would become more directly involved in oil production, and it represented a creative solution along the lines of what Norway had achieved with its hydro interests. The policy went to cabinet later that year and the NPC was authorised on 10 December 1968 to negotiate state participation agreements with oil companies. This so-called socialisation of oil production led to claims by oil companies that they were dealing with 'blue-eyed Arabs'.

When Norway unveiled the terms of its second licensing round the following year, it included the concept of the Norwegian state's taking a direct equity interest in oilfields. There would be no cost to the government during the exploration phase, which was funded by the companies. It was effectively a have-your-cake-and-eat-it policy, and the companies had to take it or miss out altogether. In the 1969 licensing round, the government's interest ranged from 5 to 40 per cent, although detailed arrangements remained confidential.[68] The government announced this policy even though it did not have a vehicle for putting this ownership into effect. This early, though very significant, experiment with the concept of state participation in oil development would remain a central part of Norway's policy development for decades to come, and it was one that would prove to be very profitable indeed.

BOOTS AND ALL

When the American oil companies began arriving en masse in Norway from the mid-1960s onwards, they adopted what might be described as a boots-and-all approach. Companies such as Esso, Mobil and Amoco ran their global empires a lot like the way the US army was fighting in Vietnam at the time, bringing a vast array of supplies from home. In Norway, just as with every other country, the oil companies weren't very interested in looking to the local market for supplies. They specified that almost everything to be used on the platforms had to be American-made, because that was the way they had always done business. The Americans were among the global leaders in oil industry technology so this bias made sense in some respects, but the specifications went much further. The companies even stipulated that the boots the oil workers wore on the Norwegian platforms had to be American-made.[69]

The Americans had demanded in Norway and around the world that they be given unrestricted market access not only for their oil companies, but also for the supply and services industry that followed on its coat-tails. The UK government sought to address local industry and community concerns with a policy called *Full and Fair Opportunity for UK Suppliers*. This initiative reflected what one Aberdeen church minister said about the lack of onshore benefits from North Sea oil: 'The only things that we are supplying oilmen with are whisky and whores.'[70]

The US government protested vehemently against the UK policy and worked to have it killed off. The government wrote to the British Foreign Office in March 1973 and asked for the policy to be dropped and not replaced by similar measures. It also protested the link between sourcing of supplies and future drilling rights. If the UK did not withdraw the policy, the US government threatened to make it an issue under the General Agreement on Tariffs and Trade.[71] The Foreign Office responded in May that year by assuring the US government that price, quality and delivery terms were the 'principal criteria' used in the UK, indicating that the policy would not have a real effect. The Foreign Office told the US government representative that there would be no discrimination between British-owned businesses and foreign businesses that were based in the UK.[72]

There's no evidence of such an aggressive lobbying approach by the oil companies or the US government in Norway, perhaps because they would have known that Norway's firm stand would doom any such attempts to failure. In fact, the US embassy in Oslo confirmed in a 1975 brief that in relation to local contracts, 'oil companies have generally been anxious to demonstrate their willingness to cooperate with the Norwegian government and to operate as good corporate citizens in Norway'.[73] It noted that government departments were calling the foreign oil companies in to meetings to closely review their procurement practices. 'Government is understood now to be exerting real pressure to swing as much as possible of the business, especially big items, to Norwegian companies,' the cable added.

The newly arrived American businesses in the North Sea wanted to be even more prescriptive than mere supplies – Big Oil wanted to design oilfield production in a way that suited its interests rather than those of the host country. In Norway, however, its so-called industrial aristocracy,[74] a powerful group of politicians and advisers strongly influenced by Jens Christian Hauge, decided from the outset that things were going to be different in three fundamental ways. First, the government made clear that companies would have to generate business for local companies if they wanted to secure exploration and development concessions in the future. Norway found a very effective way to put the spotlight on local procurement practices – its parliament became directly involved in approving concession awards, and this review process provided much greater scrutiny of the way the multinationals were operating in Norway.[75] In the Norwegian parliament, known as the Storting, members are seated according to their region rather than party affiliation, and the role of MPs in approving concessions became a powerful driver for ensuring that oil companies engaged businesses in the regions. The policy wasn't entirely protectionist, although the Norwegian foreign ministry had concerns about its implications for free-trade agreements.[76] Second, the government would adopt a hands-on approach to field development, which meant directing the companies on how to design the platforms and how and where to build pipelines for downstream processing in Norway. From the outset the government passed a royal decree in 1965 stating that where possible, petroleum resources should be landed in Norway in order to drive downstream development. Third, the government would become a direct equity partner in profitable oilfields, often securing an interest of 50 per cent or more, which in turn gave the government even more influence over local procurement and project design.

The Norwegian business community's concern about missing out on oil-related contracts didn't just reflect their fears about the biased practices of the big multinationals; they had good grounds to believe that the oil boom would worsen their competitiveness. That is, Norwegian engineering and shipping businesses that were sidelined by the oil giants would also see their operations made even less competitive by rising labour costs and a rising exchange rate caused by the influx of money from oil extraction, as had happened in many other countries around the world. The experience of Holland was very much at the forefront of Norwegian thinking at this time. These two ill-effects now characterise what's widely known as Dutch disease, since it was first seen in The Netherlands after the discovery of North Sea oil. A third channel is inflation caused by government and consumer spending of windfall resource revenue. As the prominent businesswoman Gunvor Ulstein explains, Norwegians were aware of the misfortune experienced by The Netherlands during the early phase of its oil boom and concerned about the impact this wealth influx might have on Norwegian industry. This created a strong consensus in Norway in favour of the government intervening to ensure that local business did not miss out. 'With the Dutch disease,

Norway had seen this was not a good way to manage that raw material. That was quite important for achieving the consensus.'[77]

But for Norway's industrial aristocracy, a pro-Norwegian procurement policy and equity participation weren't going to achieve the kind of local industrial development that they had in mind. Norway had a tradition of operating large state businesses that delivered social and economic benefits to the country, and so it soon became clear that such an industrial champion would have to be created if the country had any hope of standing up to the might of Big Oil. While many other countries around the world had set up state oil businesses, Hauge and his peers had in mind a powerful state entity that could both drive local industry engagement and secure an additional source of oil profits for the state.

THE VISION THING

The early 1970s was a time of great expectations for Norway and, unlike in the period of fruitless prospecting in the mid-1960s, the discovery of oil generated growing debate and interest among the population at large. Ministers and politicians wanted to learn about this new industry and began attending late-night briefings at the Ministry of Industry. The most enthusiastic attendee at these sessions was the centre-right prime minister, Per Borten, who was PM from 1965 to 1971. He ordered all members of the cabinet to attend briefings given by the small team at the Ministry of Industry, which usually started around 5pm and would sometimes go to 10pm in the evening. Borten was keenest of all to learn, and he often stayed behind for another hour after the others had left. Parliament's Standing Committee on Industry also began coming to these briefings, recalls Gulnes.

Borten's government engaged in much discussion and report writing about this new industry. Parliament's Standing Committee on Industry began working on a white paper that laid out a broad framework for policy development for decades to come. By the time the report came out in June 1971, a new Labour government had won office, but everyone agreed on the broad strategy so the transition was seamless. The episode showed the advantage of engaging in bottom-up policy development that involves all members of parliament. The watchwords in the white paper for the country's approach were control, state participation and involvement of local industry. The report included ten key principles for achieving these aims, which soon became known as Norway's 'Ten Commandments' (see Appendix A).[78] Most of the principles sounded rhetorical, like the demand that petroleum resources be used to promote new business activity, but some of them had major implications for the way oil companies were to operate in Norway and the extent to which the government was to call the shots. Decades before concerns about climate change emerged, and when petroleum was abundant and cheap, Principle 5 banned the flaring of gas except during test periods. Principle 6 stated that petroleum from the Norwegian Continental Shelf 'must, as a main rule, be landed in Norway', except in special circumstances. This principle meant that low-cost methods such as loading oil onto tankers at sea might not be an option for future developments. It foreshadowed costly infrastructure investment in pipelines to bring the oil onshore and drive local industry development, and it really meant that it would be the government, not the companies, that would decide how fields would be developed. Principle 8 put into effect the Norwegian government's desire to be directly involved as an industry player, stating that 'a state-owned oil company be established to safeguard the State's commercial interests, and to pursue expedient cooperation with domestic and foreign oil stakeholders'. Finally, Principle 9 indicated that Norway would use its resources to develop the remote north of the country.

Norway was in a good position to capitalise on these aims, as it had a critical mass of manufacturing and a highly skilled workforce tied to its hydro and shipping industries. Manufacturing represented almost 25 per cent of GDP at the time and was the largest industry sector in the country, more than three times the size of agriculture, forestry and fishing combined.[79] Norway put very strong emphasis on skills development and employment generation, reflected in its very low unemployment rate of around 2 per cent, which was the lowest in the OECD. As Gunvor Ulstein points out, the government's policy of Norwegian preference would not have worked had the country not had such a highly skilled workforce.

The task of creating new institutions and implementing the strategy in the industry committee report fell to the Labour Party, which won office at a crucial juncture. It was March 1971, just three months before the Ekofisk field would come onstream, and the new government became a catalyst for industrial strategists to put in place a regime designed to transform the way business would be done on the North Sea and in Norway itself. The influence of Milorg resistance army veterans rose to the fore at this time with the appointment of Finn Lied as industry minister. Lied was a contemporary of Hauge from their time in Milorg and the two worked together very closely on industry policy. Lied, who had served as a Milorg captain during the war, was a trained engineer who worked at the Norwegian defence research establishment known as FFI. When Lied looked for a new undersecretary, he found a 38-year-old economics and law graduate, Arve Johnsen. After graduating from university in Oslo, Johnsen had won a Fulbright scholarship in 1959 to undertake a master's in economics at the University of Kansas, where he gained some powerful insights into how America's oil barons had made their fortune. Johnsen was raised in Norway's rural south, the son of a station master. His father worked his entire life for the Norwegian State Railways, starting off as a messenger boy before becoming a station master in the 1960s. The family of five raised pigs, hens, goats and rabbits to support the father's income. It was anything but maritime, yet education proved the key to Johnsen emerging as an industrial strategist who shaped his country's development. Johnsen, who also had a background in the Labour Party, was working for the partly state-owned hydro company Norsk Hydro, as the head of marketing for its aluminium business, when he was recruited.

Arve Johnsen, the industrial strategist. Photo taken during his time at the helm of Statoil. Image courtesy of the Norwegian Petroleum Museum.

At this time, Hauge had no official role in the government led by Trygve Bratteli, but he emerged as an influential industry strategist-cum-Svengali. Both Lied and Hauge had strong views about the importance of building up state institutions to bolster both the country's national security and its economy, and this included the role of a state oil business to drive industry development and extract an extra share of the profits generated by oil production. Both understood the significance of securing onshore infrastructure so that the processing was done in Norway, even though such development would involve the laying of hundreds of kilometres of deep-sea pipelines.

The industry committee report had given the green light to set up a state-owned oil business, as many Norwegians such as Hauge had wanted. This wasn't a particularly novel idea, as other oil-rich countries around the world operated such businesses, including BP and the British National Oil Corporation in the UK, ENI in Italy and Elf in France, but the aim of Hauge and Lied went far beyond the way these companies operated. Their aim was not socialist, says Ryggvik, and state ownership was not 'a goal in itself'. The main idea was to ensure that 'the greatest possible share of the economic rent ended up in the hands of the state'.[80] To achieve this end, the as yet undefined enterprise would become a driver of local industry involvement and investment in technology.

At first Hauge, Lied and Johnsen thought that the semi-government company Norsk Hydro could be the vehicle to achieve this goal, as the company had already taken an equity stake in exploration consortiums, including the Ekofisk field. They commissioned a local bank to secretly acquire a parcel of shares in order to lift government ownership of Norsk Hydro above the 50 per cent threshold. Informed by Johnsen's experience working at Norsk Hydro, however, they soon realised that they needed to create a completely new institution from scratch.[81] So they worked inside the government to convince key players that Norway needed an entirely new state business, a move that would require parliament to pass a law to create such an entity.

In July 1972, about one year after the Ten Commandments were handed down, the parliament voted unanimously in favour of a tripartite model that would determine the way the oil industry would operate and be regulated in Norway for decades to come. The law created a new regulatory authority called the Norwegian Petroleum Directorate (NPD) that would operate independently from the new Petroleum Ministry, which was carved out of the industry department. The geologist Fredrik Hagemann, part of the three-man nucleus of the oil administration from 1965 onwards, was appointed as the first director general of the NPD, a position he held for the next twenty-four years. The NPD would have direct oversight of operations on the Norwegian Continental Shelf. A third institution would be the state oil company called Den Norske Stats Oljeselskap A/S ('the Norwegian State Oil Company'), or Statoil for short, which would act as both an equity owner and operator (head contractor) of oilfields. Significantly, the state oil company would not be an overarching behemoth that also regulated the industry, as it was in other countries. It would be answerable to the NPD.

Statoil was formally incorporated as a limited liability company at its first annual general meeting on 18 September 1972. Its share capital of just 5 million kroner (US$770,000[82]) was divided into 50,000 shares. Johnsen was its first chief executive (and very first employee), and Hauge became its first chairman. But it soon became clear that Statoil would need much more capital, and so the government increased its funding in May 1973 to 150 million kroner ($26 million), even though the company still had only fifty employees by the end of that year.[83] The legislation to create Statoil was left vague and broad-ranging, perhaps deliberately so, and it gave the enterprise a great deal of freedom to find its own role.[84] Statoil's constitution allowed it to operate in all facets of the industry, defining its functions as 'to search for and extract, transport, refine and market – alone or in association with other companies – petroleum and related products, and to carry on other activities naturally related thereto'. The government saw Statoil's role as one of becoming an independent operator of oilfields 'as soon as possible', even though the country had very little petroleum expertise, and its aims involved a brazen plan to supplant the oil foreign companies. The government wanted private businesses, whether Norwegian or foreign, to be involved in exceptional cases *only*.[85]

It soon emerged that the creation of Statoil and the policy of carried interest, which was a form of equity participation, meant that the government had an inside running on every oil development on the Norwegian Continental Shelf. Under the policy, the Norwegian state would be entitled to take up a share of any profitable venture, without having to outlay the cost of the exploration program. Within a year of Statoil's formation, its executives would turn up at meetings at the NPD when foreign companies were discussing their exploration plans and demand to see the seismic data they had generated.[86] Kåre Willoch, who would serve as prime minister in 1981–85, soon began raising fears about this powerful entity and said that its privileged position made it a 'state within a state'.

The aftermath of the 1973 OPEC oil shock, when Arab oil producers slashed production and triggered a quadrupling in oil prices, proved to be a pivotal time for this new oil-rich nation. Ekofisk production was starting to ramp up to around 60 million barrels of oil a year, delivering a significant boost to the government's coffers, and a second major discovery followed immediately after the oil shock. The Norwegian state had taken a direct equity share in blocks won by Mobil that abutted the boundary with the UK. Drilling on these blocks began in the dead of winter in December 1973, and Mobil declared the discovery a few months later. It turned out to hold even more oil than Ekofisk, 3.5 billion barrels of oil and 77 billion cubic metres of gas.[87] The field that became known as Statfjord underscored the wisdom of securing the median line in negotiations with Britain because it actually straddled the border, with 85.47 per cent allocated to Norway and

14.53 per cent to the UK. Had Britain secured a boundary influenced by the shape of the seabed, as the Norwegian negotiators had been expecting, it could have secured this entire mammoth field. Statfjord put Statoil in the driver's seat as a result of the carried interest policy, which gave the company of about 100 employees a 50 per cent interest in one of the world's biggest offshore oilfields. Further, within ten years, Statoil had the option of becoming the production operator, which would give it even more influence over contracting. The Norwegian government secured all of this while not having outlaid any money on the exploration campaign. Mobil had to settle for a share of 15 per cent, while Esso and Shell were awarded 10 per cent each and Conoco 11 per cent.

Johnsen and his small team suddenly found themselves in partnership with US multinational Mobil. In seeking to exploit the relationship, Johnsen's main priority was to arrange for as many Statoil staff as possible to work closely with Mobil so that they could build up 'real technological know-how' and therefore counterbalance Mobil's dominance.[88] As suitably qualified Norwegians were hard to find, Johnsen had to travel to the United States to recruit technical staff who had no links to Mobil.

The Statfjord discovery coincided with a period of political turmoil linked to Norway's possible membership of the European Economic Community (EEC), and there was also growing debate over how the country was going to manage its apparently large oil wealth. While bureaucrats like Jens Evensen had been able to push through the policy framework for the early licensing rounds with little debate in parliament, there was now much public discussion about the overall strategy for oil development. After introducing the major reforms of 1972, Labour lost office when the EEC vote went against it. It was replaced by a government led by the centre-right Christian Democrats, which commissioned two major reports that further defined how Norway would manage its oil industry. The finance ministry's White Paper No. 25, *The Role of Petroleum Activity in Norwegian Society*, released in June 1974, outlined a detailed strategy for moderate development in order to make oil production as Norwegian as possible, and to use oil to fundamentally improve society.[89] The timing of this report was prescient, as it was released just after OPEC had quadrupled the price of oil to around $10 a barrel, and followed shortly after by Mobil's declaration of the Statfjord discovery. As Ryggvik has put it, this was Norway's zeitgeist moment. The report was almost entirely the work of one man, 42-year-old economist Per Schreiner, who at the time was the planning director in the Ministry of Finance. Schreiner conceived of the idea that oil revenue had a very different macro-economic impact than other types of government income and therefore the government had to exercise strong control over the industry. The key idea in Schreiner's thinking was that oil income, also known as rent, was not an ordinary economic activity and therefore it had to be managed differently. White Paper 25 evolved from this conceptual understanding.

In order to control the industry and benefit fully from it, White Paper 25 called for a 'go slow' approach. It advocated 'a moderate pace of extraction of petroleum resources', and nominated a production limit of 90 million tonnes of oil a year, or about 1.8 million barrels a day. Economist Petter Nore says that while the limit seemed arbitrary, 'it was extremely well formulated', and he credits Schreiner for conceiving of this idea. 'It was the first time anyone had globally made the connection between the oil extraction rate and the macroeconomic impact in an oil-producing country,' he says.[90] The report also called on the government to use the nation's petroleum wealth to 'develop a qualitatively better society'. It advocated in favour of developing democratic and transparent institutions that could have full control of petroleum policy. The report amplified the Ten Commandments by emphasising the need to control resource development after discoveries had been made:

Democratically elected institutions must have full control of all important aspects of petroleum policy: exploration, rate of extraction, safety measures and localisation. In order to regulate the level of production, it is necessary, however, also to develop regulatory measures, so that the extraction operation itself is brought under control after a find has been made. One appropriate method of control might be to delay the development (build-up) of individual finds. This will be facilitated by increased government participation in the activities of the Shelf.[91]

The finance minister, Per Kleppe, agreed with these sentiments and said that instead of seeing oil as a resource to be plundered as quickly as possible, it should be viewed as though it were money in the bank. 'A gradual rise in the relative price of petroleum would represent interest earned on these untouched assets,' he said.[92]

At this pivotal moment, White Paper 25 endorsed the government's view that private operators on the Norwegian Shelf would be the exception rather than the rule, thus the preference of Schreiner, and Norwegian society generally, in favour of state ownership. The finance department officials weren't trying to impose socialism on Norwegian oil production; they saw state enterprises as a tool for extracting a greater share of the economic rent. The white paper said:

Norwegian authorities have full rights of disposal over oil and gas resources, and it is their responsibility to ensure that these resources are used with due care, both with regard to Norwegian interest and in an international context. Private enterprises, Norwegian or foreign, may be engaged at the exploration and production stages and will receive suitable compensation for their efforts. But in future they should obtain the right to exploit these natural resources *in exceptional cases only* [emphasis added]. The organisational pattern for Norwegian petroleum operations must provide

Norwegian authorities with full control of all stages in the operation: exploration, production, processing, exports and marketing.[93]

The go slow approach was evident when the subsequent licensing rounds took effect. After the first round, in 1965, which released seventy-eight blocks, the second round four years later issued only fourteen blocks, and this was followed by a further eight in 1974, when the third round was launched. The fourth round was delayed by two years and was not launched until 1979.[94] Evidently, the Norwegians realised they were onto something very big and they had time on their side.

The level of political interest and planning in Norway contrasts greatly with what was happening in Britain at the same time. Even though the UK government had high hopes of benefiting from an oil bonanza, the British people viewed the oil boom with 'almost complete public indifference', according to the Scottish historian Christopher Harvie:

> This was a reticent revolution ... unlike the railways, the oil boom in the UK didn't inspire the populace; there were no encyclopaedias produced about oil like there were about the equipment, organisation and running of the British railways. An oil rig was a Meccano construction but no such toys were inspired by the oil boom. [The boom inspired] a handful of mentions in the autobiographies of responsible politicians, and silence from the politician who benefited most from it: Margaret Thatcher. At most a page of treatment in the standard histories; and save for a brief moment of consciousness in the mid-1970s, almost complete public indifference.[95]

Norway's methodical and long-term thinking contrasted with a dearth of analysis on the other side of the North Sea. Norman

Smith, who had a decade's experience in financing oil projects before working in senior civil service roles, says that references to the North Sea generally in British cabinet documents were 'conspicuous only by their absence' during the 1960s[96]. Most of the discussion in cabinet in the 1960s was about switching from coal seam gas to natural gas, and how this would require new infrastructure and mass conversion of appliances, says Smith. Academics Lind and Mackay also noted that the extent of Norway's debate and analysis stood out 'in marked contrast to similar reports in the UK, which are more notable for their virtual non-existence'. At the time, the UK was under pressure to boost oil production and address a crippling trade deficit, so the country was rushing to develop its resources. Lind and Mackay added:

> In the UK the written documents to the government usually consist of an annual report by the Department of Energy (the 'Brown Book') which is essentially a factual account describing what has happened in the North Sea in the last year ... Policies are rarely discussed in these reports and, if so, only retrospectively. The discussion of future policies in parliament, for example, occurs largely in a vacuum of published material, which has clearly hindered the consideration of alternatives. In Norway, in contrast, in addition to these occasional parliamentary reports, both the Oil Directorate and Statoil produce very detailed annual reports – much more extensive than their UK equivalents.[97]

While Norway's extensive research and analysis may have led to delays in decision making, it also meant that its oil development involved 'more democratic discussions and decisions', and this process helped the country to avoid the mistakes made as a result of rushed decisions in the UK.[98] From the outset, the Norwegian government fully acknowledged it was dealing with a non-renewable resource, and as the finance ministry explained in its landmark report, the resources belonged to the people: 'Norwegian oil policy is based on the principle that our petroleum resources belong to the nation and should be developed under full national control as an integral development of the nation as a whole and with due emphasis on the aspect of conservation of the non-renewable resources.'[99]

The extent to which Norway was able to develop a strategy for the future was a reflection on the capacity of the country's civil service at this time and in subsequent decades. These civil servants had the confidence of the cabinet, the parliament and society generally. Nore, who worked for the World Bank before running Norway's Oil for Development program in 2007–12, says Schreiner, and others who followed, exemplified this tradition. He explains: 'When other countries want to learn what is the secret behind the Norwegian success in avoiding the "resource curse", I always point to Norway's civil servants. They have been competent and non-corrupt. They symbolise the pure Weber example of a perfect bureaucrat. There has never been one single example of irregularity or corruption relating to the national civil service in the oil and gas industry. The sad thing is that there are very few developing countries that have access to the same resources.'[100]

WATCHING THEM DRIVE

One of the very first initiatives put in place by Arve Johnsen at Statoil was a program to send promising young recruits on secondments with foreign companies that had stakes in oilfields, most of which were American. Norway was trying to learn as quickly as possible, and much of its early focus was directed towards Houston-based companies that had fields in production or development, although some secondees went to companies with small interests in fields that may not be developed for many years. It was a case of using every kind of possible connection that the country had. Johnsen used the anecdote of back-seat driving when he explained to staff the approach they had to take when working with foreign oil companies. 'First, we sit in the back seat and watch them drive. Next we move into the front passenger seat and put a hand on the wheel and the gear stick, and then we move over into the driver's seat.'[101] Johnsen and the Norwegian leadership at large had a much grander vision than merely controlling upstream production.

The secondment program was part of a broader strategy within the government to rapidly expand technical and tertiary training for Norwegians so that they had the skills to benefit from this industry. Unlike the UK, which was slow to change its tertiary education sector, Norway shifted almost overnight from geology courses about rocks and minerals to petroleum geology and engineering. The technical college in Trondheim, in the country's mid-north, began turning out petroleum engineers at a rapid rate, and the universities in Bergen and Oslo switched from teaching geology courses focused on dry-land formations to oil-bearing rock formations found offshore. But in the UK, its prestigious universities were slow to offer courses in petroleum engineering. The school most interested in this industry, Imperial College London, had a course in petroleum geology, but there was no chair of petroleum engineering in the early 1970s. Nor were there any courses in offshore engineering, according to Smith. It wasn't until the mid-'70s that leading universities offered chairs of petroleum engineering. 'By then, the oil and gas industry had been active in the North Sea for more than ten years. Academically qualified manpower in specific offshore disciplines was thus initially almost non-existent,' says Smith.[102]

Norway's expansion of tertiary education certainly changed the life direction of Einar Hangeland, who had planned to become a dentist until he saw a newspaper advertisement about a new course in petroleum engineering after leaving school in the early '70s. Instead of pulling teeth, Hangeland spent the next forty years working on a whole range of oil and gas developments in the North Sea, in other parts of Europe and in the US. He was at high school during the late 1960s and had taken a keen interest in the exploration work underway off the coast of Norway. He can even recall the name of the vessel used by Esso to drill its exploration well, the *Ocean Traveller*, and wrote his high school thesis on the new era of oil and gas development in the North Sea.[103] Hangeland says the country reacted quickly to the new opportunities by opening up high-level courses to train Norwegians. 'Norway is a country that has a lot of sea towards its continental border, and we are a shipping nation by history, so there were a lot of companies and institutions that saw a role in this coming industry. Universities in Oslo and Bergin had graduated geologists and geophysicists for years and they converted,' he says. While studying, Hangeland got his first experience of work on North Sea oil rigs, which at the time involved very little health and safety training, unlike the procedures in place today.

After graduating, Hangeland worked for a research institute and then secured a job at Statoil in 1977. He worked as a petrophysical engineer, a job that involved scientific analysis of oil samples in a laboratory and on oil rigs. He spent about a quarter of his time offshore. As a fresh-faced trainee, Hangeland had his first experience of sitting through a storm that lasted two days. Even though the platform was twenty-five metres above sea level, the waves lashed the windows. 'It didn't feel unsafe,' he says.

At the time of his joining Statoil in 1977, Hangeland says he was imbued with the company's strong ethos that reflected the influence of Johnsen. The company had just 300 employees, who all understood that the ultimate aim in these early days was to turn Statoil into a very big company. 'It was quite obvious to us all that Statoil was founded by the Norwegian government to be a very strong instrument in the upcoming industry. This was explained when you were employed. What was the purpose? To become a big company.'

In these early years, Statoil's employees knew they had much to learn and that this would involve working very closely with the big oil companies with decades of experience. They showed a great deal of deference to these big players even though their motivation in so doing was to acquire the know-how so that Norway didn't have to rely on them. 'We had respect for the companies that had long experience. We were very eager to learn fast and pick up what was necessary, to become a real oil company quite fast,' he says.

Hangeland became one of Statoil's very first secondees to the US. After just two years at Statoil he found himself in Houston, Texas, where he and his new wife, AnneBethen, were sent to learn about the American oil business. The Hangelands had been married for just one month when they arrived in Texas on a Saturday in October 1979 and checked into a motel. Hangeland reported for work on Monday and was told he would be working on a drilling rig for the next week, leaving AnneBethen in the motel on her own.

For the next two years he spent a considerable time travelling around the US, often sleeping in cars in remote areas. He was assigned to work with the mid-size oil company Superior Oil, which had taken a 5 per cent stake in the newly discovered Troll field, one of the world's largest gas fields. Superior was acquired by Mobil in 1984, which then became part of the giant ExxonMobil. Working in onshore oil production was completely different to the North Sea. 'The smaller scale than the North Sea made it quite easy to get an overview. In the North Sea if you asked for a new well to be drilled you would get the results three to four months later. In onshore in the States, you drill the well and if it was commercial you put it onstream almost immediately,' he says. Even though the onshore oil business in the US was not as technologically challenging as the North Sea's offshore industry, Hangeland learned a great deal: 'I learned about project-type things, how you developed a project. I learned the importance of communicating precisely. That was a very focused area in Superior Oil – communicating what you had in mind, the importance of writing and speaking precisely,' he says. Upon returning to Norway at the end of his secondment, Hangeland gave presentations to the board on what he had learned and submitted a report on what he had been doing in the US over the past two years. The experience in the US certainly gave him the skills he needed to move rapidly up the ranks of Statoil over the next four decades, in roles that included negotiating pipeline agreements with Germany.

learning from other countries [handwritten marginal note]

PIPE DREAMS

Norway's plan to build pipelines linked to onshore processing plants also shows the power of education, as it was strongly influenced by Arve Johnsen's studies in the US more than a decade earlier on the Fulbright scholarship. One of the courses he took was called 'Advanced American Economic Development', which in part covered American petroleum history, including the rise of J.D. Rockefeller and Standard Oil.[104] The key insight that Johnsen gained was that Rockefeller's control of the rail networks and pipelines from the Pennsylvania oilfields – rather than primary production alone – had been the source of his immense wealth. At the time he took this course in 1960, there was no prospect of Norway's discovering oil, but a decade later Johnsen remembered what he had learned and was determined to apply the same principle in the North Sea – at the expense of American oil companies. Applying the Rockefeller approach to Norway would involve creating state-owned businesses that could own the pipelines and the plants.

A major obstacle in the way of realising this ambition was the Norwegian trench, which dropped down to 360 metres between the Ekofisk field and the Norwegian coast. When the Norwegians had first raised the plan of piping Ekofisk's oil and gas to Norway, the Phillips Petroleum executives cited the depth and ruggedness of the trench as a key obstacle. The Ministry of Industry set up the Ekofisk committee, which eventually agreed with Phillips to land the gas at Emden, West Germany, and the oil at Teesside, UK. These pipelines went down to depths of just sixty to seventy metres.

Johnsen could see that Phillips looked set to do a Rockefeller on Norway, because its pipeline could become the trunk line for future oil developments, so he proposed that a dedicated company be established to operate the pipelines, with Statoil having a 50 per cent share ownership.[105] Jens Christian Hauge, who had created a state-owned pipeline company, Norpipe, put the proposal to William Martin, Phillips vice president, who later became the chief executive of the company. Martin was visibly shocked by such an audacious move and shouted, 'This is immoral!'[106] Evidently, the company was unaccustomed to such boldness from other countries. Hauge remained calm and measured as Martin fulminated, and simply asked him to provide a legal basis for this assertion. Martin was unable to do so. The demand was at odds with the provisional agreement negotiated between Phillips and senior industry department officials, who believed that a modest 10 per cent share of the pipeline business after two years would be a fair arrangement.[107] Phillips caved in because it realised it could not afford a lengthy delay, and the Ekofisk field was so big that it was going to be very profitable even without control of the pipeline. As a result, Norway got a foot in the door of the pipeline business even though it had failed to secure onshore development with its first big field. This was an important first step towards achieving much grander designs down the track.

4

THE PRICE OF PROSPERITY

'Whatever precautions are taken, there'll be a disaster in the
North Sea, sooner or later.'

Texan oilwell firefighter Paul 'Red' Adair

THE WILD WATERS OF THE NORTH SEA COULD HAVE BEEN
mistaken for a war zone during the early phase of oil development, given the loss of life that occurred. Even though the
government had wanted to put a brake on development with its 'go
slow' approach, companies were risking lives as they raced ahead
in a bid to recover their massive capital outlay. Regulators were
unable to keep up with the frenetic activity. In the Norwegian sector alone, ninety-two people died in accidents relating to the
offshore facilities in the first dozen years. Helicopter crashes
caused by far the greatest loss of life, accounting for one-third of
these deaths.[108] But diving accidents and falls were also big killers.
The UK's zone was even more deadly, based on the fragmented
data made available by the government on the human toll of its
North Sea operations going back to the early years.

As a seafaring country with very little arable land,[109] Norwegians have always looked to the sea to generate wealth, which is
why they became Vikings. And this might explain why, as a people who have for millennia been accustomed to the loss of life at

sea, the Norwegians initially took these deaths in their stride. Some of the early fatalities were not reported in the mainstream media, or they generated a short inside-page story. Many of the men killed in these earlier years were foreigners, including British and South Americans brought from the Gulf of Mexico. However, nothing could have prepared the country for the scale of the losses that lay ahead.

The twenty-seven separate platforms that comprised Phillips's Ekofisk operation were by far the biggest operation on the North Sea and they proved to be deadliest of all; forty-five men died in the first six years of operations, sixteen of them in helicopter crashes. The building of the giant Statfjord platforms cost many lives when in February 1978 a fire broke out in one of the platform legs. Management responded by swiftly shutting down the flow of oxygen to the area, causing five men to die of suffocation as 700 fellow workers looked on.[110]

Divers were required to push technological limits and were among the first to die. Ten divers died in the first twelve years of operations. Diving required expensive and technically complex systems, but fatalities often resulted from human error. Some of these accidents in part reflected the fact that drilling rigs were controlled by ship owners and could be excluded from national safety laws. In 1976, six men died in an accident on the Norwegian-built *Deep Sea Driller* platform. Seven years later, five men were killed on the same drilling rig, renamed the *Byford Dolphin*, when a simple mistake led to a massive drop in pressure inside a decompression chamber.

The inherent dangers of operating in the wild conditions of the North Sea led Phillips Petroleum to embark on a mammoth engineering feat. Initially, the company had offloaded oil into tankers moored at a platform, but this could not be done in bad conditions and as a result production would grind to a halt. In order to safely and effectively produce oil from Ekofisk, the company devised a solution that involved building its own island above the field. Using a French design, local Norwegian engineering firms built the structure at Åndalsnes fjord using 238,000 tonnes of steel and concrete.[111] It was comprised of giant storage tanks that could hold one million barrels of oil, which were then enclosed within a breakwater so that the oil could be safely stored in rough conditions, thereby allowing production to run continuously. Measuring the height of a nineteen-storey building, the structure comprised a perforated cylinder designed to buffer the impact of the sea, which in turn protected tanks that were used to store oil when tankers were unable to safely access the site.[112] The structure sat on the seabed in seventy metres of water, like a giant man-made iceberg with a small tip protruding above the water line. The platform on top of the tank covered three acres and its construction in Stavanger used more steel than the Eiffel Tower and enough concrete to build a 59 kilometre freeway. At the time, no man-made structure installed on an oilfield anywhere in the world said more about the efforts – and risks – involved in extracting fossil fuel.

Swedish engineer Hans Klasson spent three years building platforms that made up the Ekofisk operation, along with parts of the storage tank. The work involved lifting steel modules into place using a crane ship. Klasson had been trained as a civil engineer to build roads and bridges, but he then found himself applying these same skills in the rugged North Sea. It was 'really hazardous work', with the weather window often as little as two to three hours a day, he says.[113] Despite the dire conditions, Phillips was pushing contractors so that production could commence as soon as possible. 'Phillips was desperate to get Ekofisk onstream so we worked right through the winter,' he says. Klasson had been working on pipeline installations in Australia when a colleague told him about the new work opening up in the North Sea. The two joined the Italian engineering firm Micoperi, which had installed a 2000-tonne crane onto an oil tanker for building oil platforms in the North Sea. Known as the M26, the vessel was the biggest offshore crane in the world at the time, recalls Klasson. Phillips had engaged Micoperi because the executives thought that it would be able to work through the rough conditions, but even so the engineers were on standby around half the time.

The man-made island was a temporary solution that preceded the building of an oil pipeline to the UK, which was completed in October 1975. Incredibly, the tanks became redundant after about a year when this pipeline was completed, but the top of the breakwater was then used to build a gas-processing facility, the world's first such facility to be built offshore. The oil pipeline allowed the company to ramp up production, making Ekofisk a dominant part of the Norwegian economy. By the end of 1976, oil production had reached 120 million barrels a year and revenue from this field alone exceeded all of the income tax paid in Norway. The value of production exceeded the output of the fisheries and agriculture industries combined. As production rose, Phillips also upgraded its estimates for the recoverable reserves to more than 3 billion barrels of oil. Gas exports to Germany commenced in 1977 after the 440 kilometre pipeline to Emden was completed. The Ekofisk operation had become the hub for six other fields developed after its discovery, all of which used the central platform for piping gas to Germany and oil to the UK.[114]

The sheer scale and complexity of this offshore industrial hub highlighted what it took to extract oil in the wild North Sea environment. Norway's tripartite regulatory model, introduced in 1972, was supposed to uphold the highest standards of safety, but in practice it proved to be patchy at times. The chief regulator, the Norwegian Petroleum Directorate (NPD), didn't have responsibility for diving operations until 1983. The NPD had a very wide brief, and workplace safety was just one of its portfolios. It had primary responsibility for licensing of blocks, as well as managing safety, emergency preparedness and the working environment of all North Sea operations.[115] In setting up the NPD, Norway's politicians were acutely aware of the dangers of lax regulation, especially as it applied to state-owned businesses. A decade earlier, twenty-one mineworkers in a state-owned operation on a remote Arctic island had been killed, and people were still talking about this accident when the oil industry began to emerge.[116] Even so, the Norwegian government mistakenly thought it had done enough when it provided resources to the NPD, but there were a few dissenting voices from the very beginning. In 1974, just two years after the NPD was set up, the head of the safety department, Arne Flikke, resigned after complaining that he did not have the resources to inspect offshore platforms on a regular basis.[117] Funding was increased, though not by enough to reach all of the platforms, of which at this time there were only a handful. Inspections alone could not guarantee against disasters at any rate, and the strict workplace culture adopted by the American firms, in which employees were reluctant to speak out about problems for fear of being dismissed, proved to be a major obstacle to fixing the problems. At times, the Norwegians did prove to be assertive. When the giant Statfjord field was being designed in the late 1970s, Norwegian officials insisted that Mobil build a separate platform for worker accommodation, as they had done with Ekofisk, in order to address safety concerns.[118] The company initially resisted this instruction, though in the end it had no choice as Norwegian regulators had the upper hand. But as was learned a short time later, oversight of accommodation facilities proved to be the Achilles heel in the entire Norwegian oil business.

A WAKE-UP CALL

Environment Minister Gro Harlem Brundtland wasn't convinced that the country had good regulation in place, and she warned her cabinet colleagues that Norway was running a serious risk of deadlier disasters. Brundtland served as environment minister from 1974 to 1979, in two Labour administrations, and her approach to addressing safety lapses became a defining aspect of her political career. She went on to become the country's first female prime minister and served three times in this role. In 1977 the Labour government developed a plan to drive exploration into deeper and colder waters north of the 62nd parallel, about fifty kilometres beyond the Statfjord operation. This parallel is about 200 kilometres north of Bergen and is well beyond the Shetland Islands north of Scotland. The plan was backed by unions and the industry, but Brundtland was not convinced: 'Within the oil industry and in broad political circles, there was a decided push to extend activities northward as soon as possible. The majority of union leaders and the population in northern Norway agreed. I had my doubts, to put it mildly.' [119]

Gro Harlem Brundtland, Norway's first female prime minister, who in the late 1970s held grave fears about the country's capacity to safely manage North Sea operations. Image courtesy of Mørland & Johnsen.

Brundtland's fears were realised on the evening of 22 April 1977, when a blow-out from Ekofisk's *Bravo* platform spewed an estimated 120,000 barrels of oil into the North Sea over eight days. Some estimates reported in the media put the real figure at four times that amount.[120] The blow-out occurred while an offshore production well was undergoing maintenance, known in the industry as a 'workover', a precarious operation at the best of times. During this operation, a blow-out preventer had been installed upside down.[121] Brundtland was attending a wedding when she received an urgent phone call at 11.55pm. It didn't surprise her. 'As an environment minister, I was less shocked about such an accident than many of my colleagues. I knew the oil drilling in the North Sea was pioneering work. I had been arguing that risks were real,' Brundtland recalled.[122]

The incident did not lead to loss of life, as all of the workers from the platform were safely evacuated, but Phillips, the NPD and the government as a whole found themselves completely unprepared for dealing with this situation. Brundtland immediately set up an 'action group' to take control. Such a group had been under 'active consideration' by the government but it was yet to be established. The group, chaired by Hans Christian Bugge, the new director of the State Body for Pollution Control, was given the authority and budget to carry out whatever action was necessary, and four days later the group was formally established by royal decree as the blow-out remained unchecked.[123] Prior to this incident, Norway had not yet worked out whether the government or the company would take operational responsibility in the event of a blow-out. 'All that had been known a priori was that the government could take over the management of the crisis if the situation demanded it,' according to an analysis of the spill published by the International Institute for Applied Systems Analysis (IIASA).[124] Brundtland's decision meant that Phillips 'became subordinate to the government even though the company was to both carry out the work and pay for the entire operation', said the IIASA paper. Norway, unlike the UK, did not put a cap on the company's liability for paying clean-up costs. Brundtland and Bugge insisted that Phillips deploy a drilling rig to the site, which was a costly move because drilling rigs were tied up on contracted work. 'This costs money, and the company hesitates, but complies,' wrote Brundtland.[125]

The action group vetoed the use of chemicals to clean up and contain the spill, instead directing that mechanical devices and flotation boom be deployed. The government had in December 1976 introduced a new regulation requiring operators to have on hand mechanical equipment – such as booms and skimmers – for cleaning up spills of up to 8000 tonnes a day, in line with the maximum spill rate of the *Bravo* platform. But Phillips was yet to comply with the new regulation and was still reliant on chemicals. Phillips continued to use chemicals for the first twelve hours before being told they were prohibited.[126]

Brundlandt flew to Stavanger the next day and then on Sunday, about thirty-six hours after learning about the spill, she joined the prime minister and industry minister on a helicopter flyover. As they approached the platform they could see the black crude oil gushing into the sea around the platform. The blow-out attracted global media attention and Brundtland was fielding questions at press conferences with more than 100 journalists, many of them from overseas. As the environment minister engaged in a relentless series of press conferences and interviews, she believed that she was defending her country's honour.[127]

The clean-up ran into further problems when it emerged that the workers hadn't been properly trained to use the skimmers, so they were able to recover only a small fraction of their rated oil capacity. It was impossible to say whether this was the result of poorly trained staff, the rough conditions or equipment failures. As the slick spread over an area of 1500 square kilometres, coordinating the boats and crews to carry out the operation proved to be unwieldy, especially as the slick broke up as it moved towards the Norwegian coastline. In all, only 800 tonnes of oil were collected, and despite this poor effort the government remained resolutely opposed to using chemical dispersants because of environmental concerns. Coastal communities began to make preparations for being inundated with oil. However, the rough conditions proved to be of some benefit as they had the effect of breaking up the slick, and by 3 May, the government claimed that most of it would disintegrate within the next five days. It then demobilised its coastal protection plans.

While these efforts were underway, Phillips flew in the American well-control expert Paul 'Red' Adair, who wore a signature red hard hat. Adair engaged another drilling rig so that it could drill a secondary well and relieve pressure, which eventually brought the well under control on 1 May, after eight full days of uncontrolled release. This was by no means a severe oil spill by international standards, but the Norwegian government set up an independent commission, which concluded that poor organisation and administrative systems for controlling well maintenance had been the cause. The government then issued its own white paper on safety for the offshore operations, which recommended improved training of oil company personnel for dealing with spills, new regulations for technical inspection and control of offshore operations, and a wide-ranging research program on emergency situations and safety.[128] Writing immediately after the incident, Hans Christian Bugge said: 'Fortunately, there was no fire or explosion at the *Bravo* blow-out and no loss of life. The blowing well was capped within one week. No oil reached the shore and no complaints were received from fisherman; it is thought that the immediate damage to the marine environment was insignificant.' Perhaps the point should have been made that Norway had been very lucky on this occasion.

Red Adair, who was played by John Wayne in the 1968 film *Hellfighters*, believed that the conditions in the North Sea were so severe, and the equipment so lacking, that there was a catastrophic accident waiting to happen. He said after the *Bravo* blow-out:

> Whatever precautions are taken there'll be a disaster in the North Sea, sooner or later. There are no proper facilities for coping with it. The thing is time, to get trained personnel there. By then, a well might have caught fire – then it gets larger and larger. The more wells you have, on any platform, the more difficult it gets, because the heat will go on to the next tree. The hardware to deal with a disaster? For a real blow-out, you don't have anything.[129]

Norway has so far been spared the loss of life through such a catastrophic fireball, but in the 1970s and 1980s there were many more ways for workers to die in what was indeed a watery Wild West.

FATALLY FLAWED

As Norway's south-west city of Stavanger boomed in the 1970s in step with the emerging oil industry, Phillips named one of the Ekofisk platforms after a home-grown great, the nineteenth-century literary giant Alexander L. Kielland. Born into an aristocratic family in 1849, Kielland emerged as a sharp social critic who raged against Norway's authoritarian school system and the excesses of the clergy, among other things. And as a Stavanger local, he also wrote about the sea. He began his first novel with a reference to the North Sea: 'Nothing is so boundless as the sea, nothing so patient.'[130]

Kielland's name was attached to the platform used to accommodate as many as 350 Ekofisk workers. The gigantic five-column floating structure, known as a Pentagone platform by its French manufacturer, was originally designed as a drilling rig for operations in rough conditions. Each of the large columns floated on massive pontoons, and the entire structure supported a deck about the size of two football fields – 101 metres long and 97 metres wide.[136] It was stabilised with horizontal support beams connected to each of the columns, and ten anchors. But as was later learned, the structure had a design flaw: it would not maintain buoyancy if one of the legs became detached. The consequences of this flaw were magnified by the company's decision to use the platform for accommodation rather than for drilling, meaning many more workers would be on board at any given time. After acquiring it in July 1975, the company progressively converted it into a floating hotel by adding Consafe sleeping modules, stacked four storeys high.[131] The health and safety regulations at the time were so inadequate that a rig designed for drilling was allowed to accommodate this many workers.

Norway's emerging inspection regime undertook full surveys of such rigs every four years, so the NPD carried out 'intermediate' inspections of the *Kielland* in September 1977, August 1978 and September 1979. But these annual inspections did not look at the horizontal bracings that reinforced the five columns, as this could only be done by raising the rig above the waterline.[132] The *Kielland* was due for a full annual survey in April 1980, though the NPD had given approval for this date to be extended until June 1981. Despite the pretence of strict regulation, companies were able to find ways to push authorities when it suited them.

On the night on 27 March 1980, as gale-force winds of about sixteen metres per second and six-metre waves buffeted the Ekofisk operation, workers retreated to the *Kielland*.[133] As an eerie fog descended on the North Sea, the *Kielland* had been winched away from the *Edda* platform and by early evening the majority of the 212 workers on board were in the mess hall and cinema. At around 6.30pm the workers heard a sharp crack, followed by some trembling, as the rig keeled over to an angle of about thirty degrees. Ola

Gaustad, a 31-year-old electrician from Trondheim in Norway's mid-north, was playing cards when he heard a large bang. Furniture went flying, lights went out, and the emergency lights came on, but they lasted only a short time.[134] One of the five horizontal supports had given way, putting the entire structure at risk of collapsing; the men had less than twenty minutes to escape.

Few men knew what to do, and no-one took command of the emergency, which meant that for most of the men on board, those precious twenty minutes were wasted. Nor did anyone think to close hatches to stop water entering the structure. Despite the rough conditions, the supervisors on board the rig had not sealed the structure by closing water-tight doors and ventilators on the columns, contrary to the operational manual, a commission of inquiry later found. This rapid intake of water led the platform to capsize at around 6.50pm, which was when the bracing cables snapped and the entire leg became completely detached. The platform turned upside down and sank, leaving only the bottom of its feet visible.[135] Most of Gaustad's fellow workers remained trapped on board when it capsized. The hallways were blocked by loose cabinets that had fallen down when the platform keeled over. The *Kielland* was equipped with seven Harding lifeboats, each with a capacity of fifty persons. Four of these were successfully lowered but three could not be released before they smashed against the platform. Only one was launched, but this involved a worker taking an axe to a cable so that it could be released.[136] Twenty-six men managed to scramble on board this boat, while a fifth lifeboat popped up after the platform had capsized and fourteen men made their way into it.

The event sparked a major international rescue operation that involved helicopters and ships sent from Scotland, Denmark and Germany, as well as Norway. As the Ekofisk operation was located just as close to the UK as to Norway, an RAF Sea King helicopter deployed from a base in Scotland was the first to arrive on the scene and locate survivors. Mike Yarwood, an RAF flight sergeant aboard the Sea King, lowered himself down on a rescue cable and plunged into the icy waters to reach a life raft with ten Norwegians on board.[137] The men had swum to the life raft that had been thrown from the nearby *Edda* platform. It took Yarwood around forty-five minutes to load each man onto the winch, as the survivors' hands were so numb they could barely hold on. Even though the Sea King captain thought that Yarwood had already exceeded 'the call of duty', Yarwood went back into action when he saw the lifeboat with twenty-six men on board.[138] Upon reaching the stricken men Yarwood assessed the situation and realised that it would be safer for them to be rescued by boat rather than winched into the helicopter. However, two Norwegian Sea Kings arrived at around 10pm and took turns to rescue these men throughout the night.[139] One survivor, chief technician Odd Osland, who waited for about twelve hours to be rescued, said many of the men had little or no protective clothing in the freezing conditions. The real tragedy of this event is that so few men were able to scramble out of the platform and reach lifeboats. The greatest loss of life occurred in the cinemas and mess hall. Only seventeen of the sixty people in one of the cinemas survived, while the survival rate in the mess hall was fourteen out of forty-eight men.

Of the 212 people on board, 123 never made it to safety: 94 Norwegians, 27 Americans and two British men died in what became Norway's worst maritime accident since the Second World War. Many of the Norwegians came from the Rogaland county around the city of Stavanger. Kåre Svendsbøe of Føresfjorden was forty-two years old at the time and lost six of his seven friends on board the platform. He still has nightmares and has been unable to work again.[140] Norwegians had become accustomed to losing people at sea over the centuries, but an accident on this scale shook the country's confidence in its affluent future and made people realise that Norway's new-found prosperity had come at a very high price.

The capsized Alexander L. Kielland *platform showing the space left by the missing leg and the four-storey accommodation quarters where many of the men died. Image courtesy of Scanpix.*

In the immediate aftermath of the event, the gruesome task of recovering bodies fell to the divers who were working on Ekofisk and nearby operations. Arne Jentoft saw several bodies on the seabed, still wearing their lifejackets as they had been sucked down by the rig when it capsized. Ten days after the tragedy, the NPD approved a request from Phillips to release eighty-five barrels of drilling mud into the sea, making visibility and the recovery task even more difficult. Divers made a written complaint and Phillips later apologised.[141]

Immediately after the tragedy, a commission of inquiry was appointed. Chaired by the district judge Thor Næsheim, the commission's other experts included a professor of marine structures, a captain and platform manager and a representative of the Norwegian Shipowners' Association. It was an entirely Norwegian panel. The five commissioners spent one year examining the incident, taking evidence from 117 witnesses. Some of these witnesses were still deeply traumatised by their experience, including one man who refused to be interviewed by the commission and police.

When it reported one year later, the inquiry's findings boiled down to four key factors behind the capsize and massive loss of life. First, faulty welding on one of the horizontal beams resulted in fractures which, combined with overloading, caused the leg to become detached. Second, the Pentagone structure was 'not designed to have sufficient stability' in the event of losing one of its columns. Third, the platform capsized quickly because water poured into the structure through open doors and ventilators in the columns.[142] Without such water penetration, the platform should have stayed upright for at least an hour, the commission concluded. Fourth, the failure to quickly evacuate the platform was the result of inadequate health and safety training. Of the 212 people on board, only 76 had undergone any form of evacuation training, and of these 50 had been trained for just one day. Despite the lack of specific training, the commission concluded that 'experience at sea' was a more significant factor in determining the rate of survival. In other words, the men who had greater seafaring knowledge and years at sea were strongly represented among the survivors, indicating that they knew instinctively that they had to evacuate at the first sign of a problem. One final decision left for government in closing this matter was what to do with the *Kielland* platform. It took three attempts over a period of three years before the rig could be righted. The government finally chose to sink it in 700 metres of water in Nedstrand fjord north of Stavanger, which in some respects only served to give oxygen to conspiracy theorists who made baseless claims about the collapse having been caused by sabotage.[143]

The inquiry showed how Norway's regulatory regime proved to be woefully inadequate in the extreme conditions. As Norwegian historians Gjerde and Ryggvik wrote in their account of these events, the tragedy was seen as the result of rushed development by individual companies that was too focused on achieving fast financial returns at the expense of safety: 'In the eyes of many Norwegians, the *Alexander L. Kielland* disaster symbolised the failure of policy based on forcing the pace of oil production, and thereby the flow of revenues to the government's coffers, without paying adequate attention to safety.'[144] Paul Bang and Olaf Thuested, who both work in senior advisory roles in Norway's Petroleum Safety Authority (which operated within the NPD at this time), said the country's safety and working environment regulations had been copied from other industries and were highly fragmented, as the creation of the NPD still meant that other regulatory agencies were involved. The Norwegian understanding of safety had its origins in the regulations of the early 1970s for fire and explosion prevention, which meant they were not specifically designed for the oil industry.[145]

In the wake of this disaster, the government introduced new safety requirements in the *Petroleum Activities Act 1985*, which encouraged greater openness and collaboration among the workers. The changes also meant that a single agency, the NPD, became the sole regulator with responsibility for drafting the detailed regulations as well as overseeing their implementation and adherence on the offshore platforms.[146] The approach became one of 'enforced self-regulation', which meant that oil companies had to exercise greater responsibility for monitoring and reporting of safety issues, rather than relying on the NPD inspectors to find faults. Operators were required by law to set up a tripartite arrangement for consultation and collaboration on safety issues, thus breaking down the American-style work culture that discouraged openness from workers. It required them to establish a 'dialog between employees, employers and government on the issues relating to development of regulations'.[147] The regulations became risk-based and had to become highly adaptive, given that technology application in the industry

Pg. 57 –
"oversight..."

was in a state of continuous development. And evacuation training became a core part of the induction of all new platform workers.[148]

This tripartite approach to collaboration was put into effect through an external reference group, established to implement safety regulations, which later became known as the Regulatory Forum, and was followed in 2000 by the Safety Forum. Finally, in 2004 the safety function of the NPD was given to a new institution to be known as the Petroleum Safety Authority (PSA), which reports to the Ministry of Labour.

In the wake of the *Kielland* tragedy, there were a further twenty-two deaths on the Norwegian Continental Shelf over the course of the 1980s, and in the 1990s the death toll rose to thirty (see Appendix B). Any working environment that involves a combination of remote location, rough seas and highly flammable petroleum is inherently dangerous. The fireball foreshadowed by Red Adair occurred in the UK sector in 1988 when a gas leak turned the *Piper Alpha* platform into an uncontrollable fireball, killing 167 of the 228 workers on the rig and nearby vessels. The fire was so great that it took three weeks to extinguish. Once again, oil companies were unable to cope with the scale of the disaster and they called on Red Adair to bring the blaze under control.[149]

5

SEABED SOLDIERS

'There are some ex-military superintendents that think they are
still in the military and that divers are an "expendable" asset.'
American diver Alan Krell, who spent fourteen years
diving on oil and gas operations in the North Sea

NORWAY LOST THE FIRST BATTLE WHEN PHILLIPS WENT
ahead and built pipelines from the Ekofisk field to the UK and
Germany, but it wasn't about to lose the war. While securing a
50 per cent share of the Ekofisk pipeline business offered some con-
solation, Arve Johnsen especially was more determined than ever to
build a pipeline across the 300-metre-deep Norwegian trench, even
though the costs and risks involved in such a project were immense,
and there was little political will within the parliament to back the
plan. Johnsen saw his role as running a military-style campaign, and
such risk was an inevitable part of capturing the 'strategic heights' in
order to secure the ultimate prize of petroleum-led industrialisation
on Norwegian soil.[150]

The *Kielland* tragedy had shown Norwegians that their new-
found prosperity had come at a great price, but the government's
ongoing contest with the oil companies would involve continued
courage and risk-taking. The foot-soldiers in this war were the
divers who, in order to win the strategic heights, would in fact have

to descend to extreme depths for three to four weeks at a time in operations that were not dissimilar to being sent to the moon. Divers were deployed in their hundreds to literally bolt and cement Johnsen's grand plan onto the seabed in water depths of 200 metres or more, and they also kept the oil platforms operating safely. As oil platforms proliferated around the North Sea, deep-sea divers were needed in ever-increasing numbers to drill or abandon wells, and to undertake regular inspections and maintenance of platforms. And they were a vital part of the teams that built the undersea pipelines, which often involved digging and cementing in water depths of 180 to 220 metres, though some went as far down as 250 metres.

Initially, scuba divers were used in the North Sea but they could safely work at depths of only fifty metres. Until the 1950s, it was believed that divers could go no deeper than 100 metres before starting to lose their minds and risking imminent death. This condition, known as nitrogen narcosis, or the martini effect, occurs when nitrogen gas saturates the blood and tissues and makes the diver feel drunk (similar to drinking a martini for every fifty feet of depth). Even more dangerous is the ascent, which causes these nitrogen bubbles to increase in size and cause great pain and often death. Also known as the bends, this phenomenon was first discovered in the 1870s when workers building the Brooklyn Bridge suffered this condition. The workers who were sent below the water level to build the pylons returned to the surface with excruciating joint pain, paralysis and convulsions, and some died. The engineer charged with building the bridge, Washington Roebling, suffered from the bends and remained partially paralysed for the rest of his life.[151]

In order to go deeper, divers went down in a small capsule called a bell, but they could only work at extreme depths for an hour at most before having to undergo decompression. This technique, known in the industry as bounce diving, proved to be a costly and time-consuming way of carrying out the massive amount of work that was needed at the time. The task of laying oil pipelines in deep water prompted oil service companies to deploy a relatively new technique known as saturation diving, which involves breathing a combination of oxygen and helium to allow divers to stay below the surface for weeks on end. Breathing this gas would make the divers sound like Donald Duck when speaking. The gas is absorbed by their body tissues until the body becomes 'saturated' with it, hence the name. Saturation diving delays the need for undergoing decompression – which restores the oxygen in body tissues to the normal level – and it means that the amount of decompression time will be the same, no matter how long the diver remains under water. In 1956, a Royal Navy diver reached successfully reached 600 feet (183 metres) using this technique, but it took him twelve hours to return to the surface. In 1961, Hannes Keller, a Swiss mathematician, used what was then a secret combination of gases to briefly reach a depth of 728 feet (222 metres).[152] An editor from *Life* magazine accompanied Keller on the dive and wrote an article about it, which sparked the interest of the US Navy and the Shell oil company. A year later, Keller went down to 1000 feet (305 metres). He sold his rights to Shell, which in turn funded a ten-year R&D program, but he also developed deep-diving systems and hyperbaric pressure chambers which he then licensed to another company. Keller, now in his eighties, also developed a computer system and other software but over the past decade he has worked full-time as an artist.

From 1970 onwards, saturation diving was deployed in the North Sea by the American diving company Taylor Diving, which had been acquired by Halliburton. Taylor had applied the technique in 1965 when repair work was being carried out in water depths of sixty metres on the Smith Mountain Dam in Virginia. The work was done in just five days, whereas using bounce diving would have taken several weeks.[153] Saturation diving meant that workers could stay down below for several weeks while working on ten- to twelve-hour shifts at a time when the industry was virtually unregulated. Norway's off-shore regulatory model still remained fragmented and diving was not supervised by the labour ministry, nor the NPD. The system involved slowly immersing divers under close observation from above to ensure they do not suffer from joint pains or other symptoms of the bends. Once they have reached their working depth, the divers transfer into the water using a diving bell attached to the saturation unit. Divers exit the bell while attached to an umbilical cord that coils around the inside of the bell. They wear a suit attached to a helmet that has communications, a demist system, hot water, various gauges and a bail-out system with five to six minutes of emergency gas. But Norwegian diver Karl Jørgensen explained how the conditions were also quite primitive as well. There was no proper toilet inside the mini-submarine, merely a bucket with a lid. And because helium made the body cold, the air temperature inside was kept at a warm twenty-nine degrees Celsius, but this also helped to spread bacteria. The men often suffered from ear inflammation and athlete's foot. After several weeks below the surface, the air inside the sat unit was foul.[154] At the end of one tour of duty Jørgensen stepped outside the unit and breathed fresh clean air for the first time in weeks. When he realised he had forgotten something, he went back inside the chamber and was shocked by the stench.

Many of the divers who took part in these deep-sea expeditions had served in the British, US and Australian navies. Like men going off to war, many of these divers were young men embarking on what they thought was a great adventure. The working environment was strict and not unlike being part of a military operation. American diver Alan Krell, who spent fourteen years diving in the North Sea, says some of the operations were run by 'ex-military superintendents that think they are still in the military and that divers are an "expendable" asset'.[155] Former Royal Navy diver Jim Limbrick said divers did exactly what they were told. 'The tool-pushers or barge captains were the bosses and their word was law,' he wrote.[156] These risks and demands produced a high casualty rate in the early years, while many more divers suffered long-term mental and physical damage. In the twelve years to 1979, ten divers were killed on the Norwegian Continental Shelf, but it was far worse in the UK sector, where there were twenty-six diving fatalities in the five years to December 1976 alone. The divergent results are probably better explained by luck for the Norwegians than anything else, given that in this time there was a similar work culture and equally lax regulation on both sides of the North Sea. But unlike Norway, which has complete injury and fatality data going back to the very beginning of its oil development, the UK does not hold comparable records. From the data the UK does have, its record looks worse, especially when helicopter crashes (which in the UK are recorded separately) are taken into account. A spokesperson for the Health and Safety Executive, which is responsible for worker safety throughout the country, says the HSE does not have records on North Sea fatalities prior to 1991 because it 'didn't assume responsibility for offshore health and safety until 1991'.[157]

The North Sea divers were well paid for their vital work, though not excessively given the risks involved. Some estimates put the salaries at about twice the Norwegian average.[158] But the money was certainly good enough to attract divers from around the world. Twelve of Norway's seventeen diving fatalities were British; one was American and the remaining four were Norwegian. The Norwegian government now admits that in this early period the diving operations were poorly regulated, and British divers claim they were used as 'guinea pigs' by the Norwegian government to advance their oil industry.

A big part of the problem was the fragmented regulatory system that allowed companies to push the limits. When the first drilling rig, the *Ocean Traveller*, turned up outside Stavanger in 1966, officials from no fewer than six agencies sought to ensure that it complied with Norwegian standards. They issued a defect notice with a list of sixty items, including radio communications, and the lack of handrails, no-smoking signs and even toilet doors.[159] This might have seemed like regulatory overkill for the crew, but it didn't always amount to an effective system of oversight, especially when companies were willing and able to cut corners to meet tight deadlines after the inspectors had vacated the scene.

Two 'frogmen' divers in wetsuits are lowered into the icy waters from the Ocean Viking rig. Image courtesy of the Norwegian Petroleum Museum.

As Phillips rushed towards first production from Ekofisk in early 1971, it pressed contractors to finish work on wells, and this involved teams of divers operating in depths of around seventy metres. In March that year, the *Ocean Viking*'s diving bell malfunctioned, so 'frogmen' divers had to continue work equipped with just wetsuits and tanks. Normally, a diving bell would be essential at such depths, but the contractor was able find divers willing to take the risks.

Two French divers who were on board went down to complete the job but they ran out of time and had to resurface for decompression. The diving operator sent a message back to Stavanger calling urgently for divers to fly to the platform. The message found Briton Mike Lally in one of the divers' haunts in Stavanger, the Dickens bar, and he was joined by Norwegian Bjørn Lilleland. Even though divers were in high demand, somehow they felt they were unable to say no when asked to work on risky jobs at short notice. 'You didn't say no when you'd first been asked. Otherwise you ran the risk that there wouldn't be a second time,' says Lilleland.[160] Lally was in no condition to undertake such a risky dive as he was seen vomiting just before plunging into the 5.9 degree waters. The 4.5-millimetre-thick wetsuits offered little protection at the water depth of seventy metres. Lilleland's mouth became so numb that he could not keep his oxygen intake in place and as a result swallowed large amounts of sea water. He was shivering violently when brought to the surface. The divers had to undergo decompression in a three-metre swell, which meant they were unable to remain at a steady depth. Lally wasn't pulled up for another twenty minutes and by the time he reached the surface he was dead. There are scant records on the cause of death, according to former Royal Navy diver Jim Limbreck. Most likely he died of hypothermia. Lally had a young family and one of the legacies from his time at the bottom of the North Sea is the hand-drawn pictures he sent to his young boy, who was still in preschool, so that he could see what his father was doing while away from home.

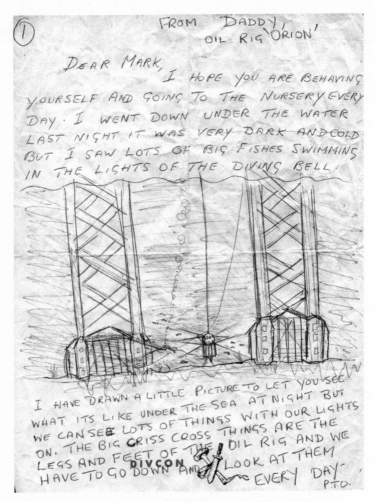

FROM DADDY,
OIL RIG 'ORION'

DEAR MARK,
I HOPE YOU ARE BEHAVING YOURSELF AND GOING TO THE NURSERY EVERY DAY. I WENT DOWN UNDER THE WATER LAST NIGHT IT WAS VERY DARK AND COLD BUT I SAW LOTS OF BIG FISHES SWIMMING IN THE LIGHTS OF THE DIVING BELL.

I HAVE DRAWN A LITTLE PICTURE TO LET YOU SEE WHAT ITS LIKE UNDER THE SEA AT NIGHT BUT WE CAN SEE LOTS OF THINGS WITH OUR LIGHTS ON. THE BIG CRISS CROSS THINGS ARE THE LEGS AND FEET OF THE OIL RIG AND WE HAVE TO GO DOWN AND LOOK AT THEM EVERY DAY. P.T.O.

DIVCON

Letter from Mike Lally to his young son Mark. Courtesy of the Norwegian Petroleum Museum.

Two months later, another British diver, Mike Brushneen, aged thirty-three, was killed when he was diving in sixty metres of water in a new type of suit that was later discontinued. Brushneen was not meant to be diving at the time because he had been promoted, and the family was planning to move back to Scotland, but the diving contractor was in desperate need of divers. According to his family, there was no accident report and no cause of death was stated on his death certificate. Within a few days of his death the family was relocated from Stavanger, in Norway, back to Scotland. Brushneen's daughter, Ann Marie McCreath, said the family heard nothing more from the company that had employed her father, and nor did it hear from the Norwegian government. Her mother raised the family in poverty. She told the BBC: 'It destroyed our family. We had very little money as we grew up. My mother lived off a widow's pension, but we got nothing from the Norwegian government. It's hard to believe that as recently as 25 years ago, these things were going on in civilized countries.' [161]

Initially, these accidents generated very little media coverage and little public interest in Norway. Norway's Directorate of Labour issued another circular on diving regulations, which was merely an update of the one issued after the first diving death in 1966. However, in September 1974 Bergen's leading daily newspaper ran a full-page article under the headline: 'The North Sea is being conquered with the lives of divers.' [162] Despite the disturbing content, the article contained no criticism of the diving companies or the government. Eventually, a commission of inquiry was held in 1975, but no single agency was given responsibility for the health and safety of divers. The Norwegian Petroleum Directorate still had no role in regulating diving.

NATION-DEFINING PROJECT

Attempting to build a pipeline across the Norwegian trench seemed unthinkable in technical and economic terms, but it was equally unthinkable for Arve Johnsen to walk away from his pipe dream. This was not a time for the faint-hearted. Johnsen decided that the giant Statfjord field would be the catalyst for realising this dream, even though the pipeline would have to plumb depths of 300 metres. Such a depth was pushing the limits of available technology and human endurance, but Johnsen was undeterred. As Statoil was destined to become the operator of this field with a 50 per cent controlling interest, Johnsen commissioned his own engineers to carry out an extensive study of the seabed, which in the mid-1970s cost a significant $20 million. The study involved sending divers to extreme depths so that the seabed could be fully investigated. Johnsen says the Norwegian authorities imposed limits and Statoil did not push them. 'We always used divers within the operating limits set by Norwegian authorities. It was not an aim to push technological or human limits beyond this,' he says.[163] The study concluded that building a pipeline at depths of 300 metres was technically feasible.

But the study didn't address the economics of a pipeline, and the plan became increasingly unpopular towards the end of the decade as building the Statfjord platforms was plagued by cost overruns and numerous technical problems. The cost of the Statfjord project had a direct impact on the national budget and on the balance of payments because it involved importing large amounts of capital equipment. While the government hadn't found a way to save its oil revenue in financial assets, it was in fact putting the money into oil and gas installations via its large equity stake in these projects. It was a costly, and risky, form of investment. As the first concrete platform, known as *Statfjord A*, inched chaotically and expensively towards completion in 1977 (it was actually still far from finished when towed into position), Norway recorded a record trade deficit of 11 per cent of GDP, reflecting the cost of capital imports.[164] National borrowing surged as the government had to fund its 50 per cent of the Statfjord development cost. Gross foreign liabilities increased fourfold compared with the level in 1970 to reach a peak at 160 billion kroner ($30.7 billion) in 1978, worth 40 per cent of GDP.[165] Parliamentarians became nervous about the scale of this three-stage development and proposed cheaper options such as using tankers rather than pipelines, which was how oil was initially offloaded for *Statfjord A*. Given the problems that Ekofisk had with tankers, it was evident that such a solution would prove unviable for this equally large oilfield, so Johnsen became more committed to securing the pipeline.

The inherent dangers involved in building the pipeline from Statfjord were there for all to see in February 1978 when a controlled dive in Skånevik Fjord – which was witnessed by doctors and other technical experts – went horribly wrong. Financed by foreign oil companies, the experiment involved three American divers being given the task of welding two pipes in a water depth of 320 metres. If they succeeded, they would set a new world record. Two divers, David Hoover and John Kohl, left the diving bell to carry out the welding but they soon ran into technical problems. On two occasions they lost hot-water supply to their suits, which meant they became very cold in the four-degree water while breathing the helium mixture. Then they momentarily lost their air supply. Kohl went into the habitat and left Hoover outside, and when he returned he saw that Hoover was lifeless. It took a full twenty minutes before they could return to the surface and Hoover could not be revived.[166] This accident prompted the NPD to finally exercise greater control of diving regulation, allotting a staff of five people. The Norwegian Labour Inspection Authority had proved to be woefully inadequate in overseeing these operations, and in investigating this incident. Its subsequent inquiry found that ten minutes of recording during the dive had gone missing, and the authority did not even request the tapes that did exist.

This incident was followed by extensive strikes by divers. The NPD introduced new regulations, which stipulated a maximum time of sixteen days in saturation and four hours in water. Finally, the government extended the *Working Environment Act* (WEA) to diving operations, but companies could still exploit the 'flag state' principle, which allowed vessels operating across boundaries to opt for a regime of their choosing. This meant Norwegian laws didn't always apply. Diving remained an inherently dangerous occupation in the North Sea, with the single worst incident in Norwegian waters occurred three years later. In November 1983, five divers who were working a drilling rig, the *Byford Dolphin*, were killed when simple human error led to an explosive loss of pressure in their habitat. Despite this tragedy, the WEA wasn't imposed on all diving operations in Norwegian waters for another decade.

The Statpipe project, as Johnsen's pipeline across the Norwegian trench became known, led to an unprecedented amount of diving activity off the coast of Norway following parliamentary approval in 1981. Statpipe involved building four separate pipelines over a total distance of 894 kilometres, at a maximum water depth of 296 metres. The cost of the project was around $9 billion,[167] making Statpipe by far Norway's biggest and costliest pipeline project. At its construction peak in the early 1980s, there were more than 800 divers at work in the Norwegian oil industry.[168] Norwegian diver Angus Kleppe, who helped to build the Ekofisk and Statpipe pipelines during a twenty-year North Sea career, says that at the time there was a great sense of pride among the divers who went down to extreme depths. Few, if any, were worried about the risks they were taking and the long-term damage that these depths could do to them. Kleppe, whose father was a Norwegian naval officer, began his career in the same navy where he did a 'hard hat' diving course that involved wearing a heavy diving outfit with lead boots and a helmet. As activity in the North Sea was gearing up in the mid-1970s, Kleppe was headhunted by the Norwegian diving firm Stolt-Nielsen Seaway, founded by the Norwegian shipowner Jacob Stolt-Nielsen.

As with the building of rigs and supply ships, foreign businesses dominated the early diving contracts, but Norwegian businesses were quick to take advantage of the opportunities presented by the huge number of diving operations off the coast of Norway. The first Norwegian diving company, 3X, got its start by studying the equipment and systems imported by the French company Comex when they were sitting on the dock in Stavanger.[169] The Norwegian shipping magnate Fred Olsen then bought the 3X business.

As part of the program for Ekofisk, Stolt-Nielsen Seaway had recruited a team of ex-navy divers from Australia to operate its boat, according to Kleppe. These pipelines were laid in relatively shallow water of sixty to seventy metres. The working environment was exacting, and not that different from Kleppe's time in the navy. He says that while there was an absence of shoe-shining, the reporting procedures and working environment were equally rigorous. Safety was constantly on their minds: 'We have typical naval discipline on how we perform our dives, all the time looking ahead to see if we were going to run into any problems. That is one big difference in how we've been working in Norway and how they are working in other places. Also a bit of influence from Australian navy divers. They were conscientious in regards to safety.'[170]

But the Statpipe project was going to be a totally different exercise, given the extreme water depth. As part of their preparation for building Statpipe these 'pioneer divers', as they became known, set a record depth of 505 metres at an onshore facility in Bergen. This gave them 'an enormous amount of professional pride', says Kleppe, who went down to 300 metres in open water as part of his preparation for building Statpipe. He adds: 'We wanted to be able to keep it up. There was an element of the heroic when divers got together and talked about what they'd achieved. It's like soldiers from different regiments when they get together to have a drink – you're all trying to tell the best story.'[171]

The lucrative contract to carry out diving works on Statpipe was secured by Stolt-Nielsen Seaway partly because of Statoil's influence, which made the company the preferred diving contractor on the Norwegian Continental Shelf. Seaway rolled out saturation diving on a grand scale after winning this contract in 1982. Kristin Øye Gjerde, who co-authored a book on diving on the Norwegian Continental Shelf, says that Statpipe involved the deepest working dives ever performed in the North Sea. Pipeline connections were made by Stolt-Nielsen Seaway in depths ranging from 180 to 220 metres, while two divers took part in the deepest operation down to 248 metres.[172] The pipeline would bring gas onshore to Kårstø, just north of Stavanger, for processing before being piped to Germany via another underwater pipeline. The extreme depth of Statpipe meant that divers had to carry out a range of manual tasks that required a great deal of brute strength.

On the water surface, the barge disgorged welded sections of pipeline while divers down below built up foundations and even did some cutting and welding. Says Kleppe: 'Our job was to inspect the pipeline as it was going along. We did pipeline support and inspections so it was laying stable. We were building the foundations for the pipeline supports and injecting concrete inside them. They'd blow up with concrete and support the pipeline.' Statpipe was laid at a rate of about two kilometres per day over a period of two years. At any given time, thirty-five to forty-five divers were in the water, and by 1983, the pipe laying had set a record for the number of diving hours in the North Sea. The human cost of this incredible engineering feat and the deep-sea diving generally was immense but, incredibly, Statpipe was built without suffering a single fatality – although divers suffered from ill-health in decades to come.

Despite the risks, the NPD's practice from 1985 onwards said that diving to 200 metres could be conducted on a routine basis, but depths of 300 metres required medical follow-up, and dives to more than 300 metres, which at the time were commonplace, had to be demonstrated to the regulator as acceptable. NPD policy at this time was as follows: 'On the basis of current technical and medical knowledge, we believe it is acceptable to dive to 400 metres.' According to Gjerde, the NPD maintained that diver intervention was essential for repairing acute pipeline damage.[173]

PUTTING ON A SHOW

American diver Alan Krell started working as a deep-sea diver in the North Sea at the age of twenty-four. At the time he started, 1988, there had been a marked improvement in safety standards in the Norwegian sector. But standards in the UK sector remained less exacting on the diving companies and this was where he had a number of close calls as a result of over-zealous superintendents who pushed divers too far. During his fourteen years on the North Sea, two of his close friends were killed.

Krell had many of the skills and attributes that divers needed to do challenging work on the seabed. He was big and strong, standing more than six feet tall, and he'd trained as a welder and done further courses in radiography and ultrasonics. He completed courses in air and saturation diving at a school in Scotland before embarking on his North Sea career. He found some of the dive superintendents ran the boats like 'boot camps': 'I've seen superintendents scream, yell and throw equipment. It doesn't get things accomplished any faster.'[174]

During his years at the bottom of the North Sea, teams of divers would spend twenty-eight days at a time pressurised to the depths to which they would be working. Each team, consisting typically of three men, took turns to work in the water for six to seven hours a day. By the time Krell arrived in Norway the government had passed exacting rules governing saturation diving, including a

21-day maximum for time spent under pressure, with severe penalties for companies that exceeded that timeline. The UK limit was one week longer, but companies typically sent divers down for twenty-eight days at a time, and they could obtain permission to go beyond this limit. Krell recalls doing thirty-two days straight in the British sector. He went down to depths of around 275 metres. Going deeper took longer and the gas mixtures became thicker. 'The gas is being turbocharged into your bloodstream,' he says. As he descended, the helium gas made it very difficult to speak. Instructions had to be spelled out slowly using military code (Charlie, Foxtrot and so on). At the end of a stint, he and his team would undergo decompression, which could last about a week. Upon reaching the surface and returning home, Krell said he felt like he had the flu for a week or more and he often suffered memory loss. 'It can take a while to get back to normal again,' he says. Memory loss was a problem for Krell and all of the divers he worked with, including those who were in their twenties and thirties. The job was also terrible for relationships. Few of his colleagues were able to maintain stable relationships, other than those who had been married for many years beforehand.

The tasks the divers carried out on the seabed could often be mundane. 'At times it was tedious, monotonous work. Where there's a problem we'd fix it.' Krell thought that often some divers did whatever the superintendents asked of them regardless of the consequences, whereas he learned from an early stage to 'put on a performance' – often making a dangerous situation seem even more dangerous in order to get supervisors to relent. But there were divers who would not question what they were told to do. He explains: 'I said to one guy, "You, know this is Hollywood. If you sense you are going to go to your death, you put on a show, you do the best you can but at the same time you have to get back to the bell alive and in one piece." Some divers didn't know how to do that.'

Survivor. Diver Alan Krell on one of his last North Sea assignments.
Image courtesy of Alan Krell.

One of Krell's close calls involved working on a boat run by one of four brothers who ran diving operations all over the North Sea. They were 'just nuts, all four of them', he says. Krell was one of only twelve ultrasonic technicians working in the North Sea at the time and he was told to do one last inspection on a weld even though there was a force-seven storm coming in. The superintendent wanted to do the last inspection so that the boat could pull off station and return to Denmark, instead of waiting another day or two to let the storm pass. During the dive, Krell's gear became entangled from the heave of the vessel in the rough swell. 'After I finished the weld scans, I looked up to see a real mess, an entanglement of down lines, messenger lines and the ultrasonic cables. The only way to quickly get the gear untangled and recovered to the deck was to cut lines. I got my knife out and cut everything. When my bell partner and I got back to the sat system I realised just how far this superintendent was prepared to push his divers.'

Another hazardous moment occurred while Krell was using a sledgehammer to bash a wellhead guide that was jammed hundreds of metres below the surface. Krell thought that the operation could 'go horribly wrong' but the supervisor told him to do as he was told. After more than a dozen strikes, the wellhead guide launched up six metres due to five tonnes or more of flotation bags that had been installed with it. Krell had just enough time to jump clear before it came crashing down.

Britons Gary Carey and Brad Westell were two of Krell's mates who went to their deaths after being pushed too far. Westell, twenty-nine, was killed in 1995 while assisting with the laying of power cables. There had not been a diving fatality in the North Sea since 1987. But the operation that claimed Westell's life looked like an accident waiting to happen. It took place at night and in a strong current, two factors that increased the risk considerably. With the tide running at a brisk rate, the slack on Westell's umbilical line became caught up in the ship's dynamic positioning thrusters, and he was then sucked into them. Westell's death was one of the very few that ended up in a UK court. The dive company was fined £200,000 for two safety breaches, and the dive supervisor was sentenced to one month's prison for perverting the course of justice after the video tapes from Westell's dive went missing. Krell says Carey was killed in August 1996 because the superintendent running the job would not take Carey's word that the well was under pressure. He was ordered to continue removing bolts, even after it was obvious that the wellhead protection cap was bleeding gas. The cap blew off, coming down on Carey. He died as a result of internal injuries. Two companies, Mobil North Sea and Cooper Cameron, were found guilty of safety breaches and fined a combined £220,000.

Krell says the attitudes and practices regarding safety in the UK and Norway diverged greatly in the time he worked in both regions. He says: 'The Norwegians were very careful. Their whole attitude was so different. If you had a team in saturation for any time over the maximum duration of twenty-one days the company in question could face severe legal ramifications. Norwegian police would have full authority to come on board and shut down the diving operation. Unless you had a damn good reason, the law is the law. They were ahead of the UK government in promoting diver safety.' He also suspects some diving companies of allowing cover-ups to occur after fatal accidents. 'There's a system in place in the UK with the diving, they push it to the limit and still wash their hands of any wrongdoing when it goes south. There are video cameras on diving helmets, [but] those tapes go missing. When Westell was killed, the dive tapes from his bell run went MIA.'

RECOMPENSE

Norway's industrial development owed a great deal to the divers, who were largely replaced by remote-controlled robots from the early 1980s onwards. Former British civil servant Norman Smith says the Norwegians switched to robotics 'far more decisively than the British'.[175] Norway suffered a further six diving fatalities in the 1980s, but it has not had once since then. Robots with mechanical arms now dig trenches, level out the seabed terrain and survey pipeline routs. Known in the industry as remotely operated vehicles (ROVs), their operators have to be qualified and recertified every year.

But introducing these machines did nothing for the hundreds of divers who were suffering the ill-effects years after their diving days ended. Angus Kleppe suffered neurological damage he believes was caused by helium bubbles. He suffers from pain and tingling in his arms, neck and head. When he drives his car for long periods, he loses the feeling in his hands. 'It's mainly aches and pains. As long as you learn to live with it, you survive,' he says. Some of his mates suffered depression and there are five he knows of who took their lives. The North Sea Divers Alliance claims that a total of twenty-three divers have committed suicide, though it is impossible to say if all were related to their time as divers.

In the late 1980s, Norwegian neurologist Kari Todnem began looking into these problems while working at Bergen's Haukeland Hospital, and her concerns led her to undertake doctoral research into the long-term health consequences for deep-water diving. Shortly after she defended her thesis, the union representatives at Stolt-Nielsen Seaway banned diving below depths of 180 metres.[174] But the Norwegian Petroleum Directorate's diving division initially rejected the findings, insisting that diving at extreme depths was harmless provided that rules were observed. The NPD was influenced by two US experts who also refuted Todnem's work – one of whom sat on the assessment committee of a leading medical journal that rejected a paper from Todnem. Another influential figure was the NPD's Olav Hauso, who still works at the Petroleum Safety Authority as a 'special adviser'.

But Todnem got her work published elsewhere. In 1991 she was the lead author of a study published in the *British Journal of Industrial Medicine* that compared the health of forty North Sea divers with that of a control group – the most robust technique for empirical research.[175] The divers had gone to depths ranging from 190 to

500 metres, with twenty-six of them having reached between 350 and 500 metres. The study found that their diving had contributed to a range of health problems relating to their central nervous system and mental function. Concentration difficulties and the sensation of tingling, pricking or burning in their feet and hands (known as paraesthesia) were common, and they had more abnormal neurological findings that were 'compatible with dysfunction in the lumbar spinal cord or roots'. They also had a larger proportion of abnormal electrical activity in their brains compared with the control group. These neurological symptoms and findings were 'highly significantly correlated with exposure to deep diving, but even more significantly correlated to air and saturation diving and prevalence of decompression sickness'. It found that 10 per cent of the divers had had episodes of cerebral dysfunction during or after the dives; two had had seizures; one had had transitory cerebral ischemia, which is caused by a lack of blood flow to the brain; and one had had transitory global amnesia. The eight authors concluded that deep diving 'may have a long term effect on the nervous system of the divers'.

Initially, the Norwegian government responded by arguing that it was not legally responsible for the welfare of these divers because it had not employed them. A 2003 report to parliament said the government had a moral responsibility to compensate them, and it responded in 1999 by setting up a program to review the health of a larger group of divers. As Kleppe explains, this step was hugely symbolic because at last 'the divers felt they'd been heard'. This study culminated in an offer of modest compensation of 200,000 kroner (around $23,000), paid between 2000 and 2002 to a group of 123 Norwegian divers who had been assessed as having 'poor health and thus reduced earning ability'. Further, the government offered payments of up to 300,000 kroner (around $35,000) to divers assessed as being in a 'precarious and acute financial situation'. The government set up Diver Contact in 2003, which was affiliated with the Norwegian Church Abroad, to provide further support, including debt counselling and other support, as well as a 24-hour helpline.

> Oil production in the North Sea is driven by strong political and socio-economic interests. The State has a comprehensive social responsibility for the petroleum activities as the property owner of subsea petroleum and, as a result of this, receives significant revenues from this activity. These diver operations have been necessary to carry out this activity, and have contributed to creating enormous values for the Norwegian society. There was little regulation of the diving activity during parts of the pioneer period, and the nature of the activity was extreme and ground-breaking. At the same time, knowledge about diving, including the equipment and methods that were used, was not as good as it is today. Therefore, the Government believes, overall, that the State must assume a political and moral responsibility for the pioneer divers in the North Sea.[176]

But these payments and gestures didn't go far enough for one hard-core group of nineteen divers. They took their case to the Norwegian Supreme Court in a bid to secure much greater compensation, but the court ruled against them in 2009 because the Norwegian state had not directly employed them. Seven British divers then took the government to the European Court of Human Rights seeking compensation of $14.5 million. The court found in 2013 that Norway had violated Article 8 of the Convention for the Protection of Human Rights and Fundamental Freedoms by failing to ensure the workers 'received essential information enabling them to assess the risks to their health and lives'. But it awarded them much more modest damages of €8,000 each.

Perhaps in response to this judgment, and the bad press that the court cases had generated, the government decided in 2014 to offer $500,000 each to certain former divers and children of deceased divers. The offer was made available to foreign and Norwegian divers who could prove they had an injury and that they were diving on the Norwegian Continental Shelf between 1965 and 1990, as well as being a member of the national insurance system at the time of the application or between the same time period. In all, 257 former divers accepted compensation. Several of these divers were foreigners, according to the Ministry of Labour and Social Services.[177]

Looking back on what Norway has achieved, Angus Kleppe thinks that the divers contributed a great deal to his country's prosperity, and that at last this has been formally acknowledged by the government. But Kleppe also thinks his country has changed, for better and for worse: 'When I was growing up there was a strong communal sense in Norway. You depended on each other. I think that might have been lost.'

6

PLANNING AND FAILING

*'We carefully plotted a course and then immediately headed in
a different direction.'*

Central bank governor Hermod Skånland, 1988

WHEN OIL REVENUE BEGAN FLOODING INTO THE
Norwegian government's coffers in the late 1970s, the
country proved just how successful it had been in reaping
the lion's share of the profits from the oil industry. Between 1976
and 1980, oil revenue increased fifteen-fold, reflecting the perfect
combination of surging production, rising oil prices and higher
taxes. There was just one problem – Norway had been unable to
agree on a plan to deal with its rare success. By the end of the first
decade of Norway's oil odyssey, the country would be destabilised
and almost ruined by a credit boom and a tsunami of oil income.

Norway had generated this income even though it had been
forced to moderate the initial proposal it had put to the oil companies at the meeting in November 1974, where the companies came
away thinking that they faced a tax of 90 per cent. But the American companies began a media campaign that lambasted Norway
for its socialist values. Together with the US government, they lobbied vigorously to overturn the tax increase. In addition to Phillips,
which was ramping up production from the Ekofisk field, Esso,

Mobil, Amoco and Conoco had interests on the Norwegian Continental Shelf. To back their case, they found some support within the Norwegian government – the Ministry of Industry, whose senior officials believed that the plan to recover a very large share of 'excess' profits was going too far. After the first stormy meeting on 28 November, a second one was scheduled for 13 December.

The American companies had considerable leverage at this time because Norway was in the middle of a licensing round. The deadline for signatures on new awards was 15 December, just two weeks after the first meeting.[178] The companies threatened to pull out of the round unless the government backed down. 'The companies say that the terms of these awards are so tough that they may not accept the blocks if the excess profits tax is also introduced,' advised the US embassy in Oslo in December 1974.[179] The embassy reported that the current proposal meant that some oilfields would return as little as 2.1 per cent of the production value to the investor. It was a game of brinkmanship and the stakes were high.

Three days before the deadline, Amoco announced that it had abandoned development of a field known as Tor. The company had already spent $15 million on finding and evaluating the field, and it blamed its decision on the proposed tax regime, but even the US State Department admitted that the field was 'marginal' and its development would be thwarted by a lack of capacity in the Ekofisk pipeline.[180] Chevron also announced it would not be taking up its award in the licensing round. Chevron had been awarded the right to act as operator of the field known as Måløy, located further north on the 62nd parallel. The powerful oil giant blamed its decision on the new tax regime, but the US State Department acknowledged that Måløy was located in deep water and its development would involve a 'high degree of risk'.[181] The Norwegian government did not look for another investor in the group that was dominated by Statoil with a 50 per cent interest and the Norwegian company Saga with 15 per cent. Amoco's decision to bail out proved to be its loss. The Tor field was taken over by Phillips and went into production in 1978, producing about 140 million barrels of oil. It remains in production today. Måløy was never developed.

In the wake of these announcements, the head of the finance ministry, Eivind Erichsen, told the assembled executive on 13 December that media reports of a 90 per cent tax take had been based on a misinterpretation, and that Norway would accept a lower overall take than the terms outlined two weeks earlier. He said: 'We now aim at a government take over the lifetime of a find which will be clearly lower than outlined in our last meeting; this will be the case for all finds.'[182] But the government was still 'not in a position to indicate a specific rate', he added. The finance minister, Per Kleppe, reassured the multinationals that the companies would be able to make a 'proper return on capital' and added: 'I understand that you have found that the suggestions made at the November meeting went beyond that point.' He then conceded that the system of base prices, 'which was supposed to cover costs and adequate profits on an average field', would be arbitrary and might prove detrimental to developing marginal fields.

But the system of norm prices was non-negotiable. These prices would be used to define the sale prices obtained by oil companies. As Erichsen explained, even though there was some opposition to this proposal, Norway needed to have a regulatory model that was easy to administer. Reading between the lines, Erichsen's big concern was tax avoidance. Norway was concerned about having to keep on top of the complex tax compliance of large numbers of oilfields. In order to avoid having to engage in costly audits and administration, Norway wanted a model that was simple and effective from a revenue-raising viewpoint. This was clearly a case of a small country with limited human resources standing up for itself. Erichsen explained further: 'On the other hand, we think you will appreciate that a country of our size must look for some administrative simplicity in dealing with complicated matters. We are therefore still convinced that a system of norm prices will be required.' The finance ministry was equally firm when it came to the distribution of dividends. Norway would not allow dividends to be deducted from the special tax; they would have to be paid from ordinary pre-tax revenue.

This was the last meeting held with the industry as a whole, and over the next few months the finance officials fine-tuned their proposal to maximise revenue and foreign investment. Early in 1975, the Norwegian government announced that it would reduce the special tax to 25 per cent, which would be paid on top of the standard corporate tax rate of 50.8 per cent. In addition, royalties would operate on a sliding scale that ranged from 8 to 16 per cent. The package included some concessions, though they were not overly generous, including depreciation at the rate of 10 per cent for fifteen years was one benefit, while a system known as 'ring-fencing' allowed companies to deduct 50 per cent of the losses from activities outside profitable fields.[183] The system of norm prices prevailed. Norway set up the Norm Price Board, which today is known as the Petroleum Price Board.[184] The Norwegian parliament put the tax regime into effect when it passed the *Petroleum Tax Act* on 13 June 1975. This new regime would rake in around 57 per cent of net profits, which was reasonably high for an offshore environment that involved considerable risks and high development costs.[185]

Britain's Labour government was watching closely as the drama unfolded in Oslo, and it finally moved to raise its level of oil taxation. Just a few days before the first Oslo meeting, the UK treasury unveiled plans for an Oil Taxation Bill that included a Petroleum Revenue Tax (PRT). But there was one vital piece of information missing – the proposed tax rate.[186] About a month after Norway's tax changes were finalised, the UK government finally went ahead with its PRT, which would apply a nominal rate of 45 per cent, but the package included generous concessions for depreciation, allowing companies to recover 175 per cent of their investment cost before paying tax, which was considerably more generous than the depreciation concessions in Norway.[187] To further assuage the oil industry, the UK introduced a safety net, which meant that the PRT would not apply in the event that it reduced the rate of return on any field to 30 per cent. Even though the government claimed an effective take of 70 per cent, the concessions offered by the government proved to be favourable for the oil companies. Shares in major UK-listed oil companies rallied on the day the changes were unveiled in March 1975. The oil sector index as a whole rose 1.6 per cent, while BP shares rose 4 per cent.

Norway's reduction in the special tax rate was a setback for its finance officials, but they weren't about to give up. Four years later, in the wake of the second OPEC oil shock, which doubled oil prices, they seized the opportunity to secure what they had originally set out to achieve. A revamped tax regime lifted the special tax to 35 per cent while it slashed concessions available to companies to reduce their taxable income. Depreciation concessions were reduced from 150 to 100 per cent over fifteen years.[188] The Ministry of Finance estimated that these changes would lift the government take to 82 per cent. The government forecast a trebling in oil and gas revenue in the four years to 1983, but in fact it did much better than that. The first platform for the country's second giant oilfield, Statfjord, started production in the same year. This additional revenue stream, combined with the new tax regime, proved to be the sweet spot for revenue maximisation. Following the exponential increase in oil revenue in the late 1970s, the government's coffers bulged even further when oil revenue more than doubled between 1979 and 1985, reaching a peak of 35 billion kroner ($4 billion).

SLUSH FUND PHOBIA

Norway's success in raking in revenue was not coupled initially with a disciplined strategy to prudently manage its oil income. It was yet to build the dam wall to divert the flood of oil revenue that it had been so successful in securing, so the country was soon overwhelmed by high inflation and a banking crisis. During the first two decades of oil discovery, Norway's economic and financial problems were on par with those of today's European basket cases, according to the current central bank governor Øystein Olsen: 'We were lucky to find oil, but then we learned some lessons. We did not go directly to the present – we learned some lessons in the '70s, we were spending a lot in the 1970s, and experienced stagflation. We had deficits higher than in Europe at the moment.'[189] A parliamentary inquiry concluded in the mid-1980s that the country showed very little capacity to avoid ending up another victim of the resource curse. This wasn't due to a lack of thought and consideration; its failure to act reflected the vexed position that the country found itself in.

Politicians and economic experts alike were intensely aware of the pitfalls that had afflicted other countries, and this situation was debated extensively from the very early days. Says Olsen: 'The consciousness of avoiding Dutch disease has been in the political sphere of Norway since the 1970s.' But despite this awareness, Norway was unable to put in place the necessary changes to deal with its new-found prosperity. As the central bank governor Hermod Skånland said in 1988, the country knew that it needed strong policies, but finance ministry officials saw the potential for creating a 'populist' fund that could be harnessed by vote-grabbing politicians and turned into a financial time-bomb that would derail the economy. So instead of taking action, the increased revenue flowed directly into the government's coffers and went out again in the form of higher government spending. In the first seven years of the 1970s, government spending increased threefold, and so did public-sector borrowing.[190] At the same time, the money supply grew at an annual rate of 20 per cent, more than double the rate of the early 1970s, thus creating the conditions for an inflationary bubble and an economic crisis.

As early as 1974, the idea of investing oil wealth entirely off-shore was first mooted, although no policy detail was discussed on how this could be done.[191] The need for such a savings strategy was underscored by the discovery of three very large fields in the late 1970s: Gullfaks was found in 1978, Troll and Oseberg in 1979. At the time of their discovery, these three fields had proven reserves of 18 billion barrels of oil, more than double the combined reserves of Statfjord and Ekofisk. Together, the three fields account for about one-third of all the known petroleum resources underneath the Norwegian shelf.

An inquiry called the Tempo Committee, chaired by Skånland, was established in 1984 to examine these issues in detail. It proposed that surplus revenue be channelled offshore before being returned to the national budget during more subdued economic times. Essentially, it advocated a medium-term fund, or what Petter Nore calls a 'buffer' fund. Nore, who was the committee secretary, says: 'We did a lot of background international work. We talked to the Kuwaitis who had set up the first big oil fund, and we talked to representatives of Alberta and Alaska who had created similar funds. We carried out innumerable macroeconomic simulations and looked at employment and social consequences of different scenarios. It was a truly fascinating time.'[192]

The Tempo Committee argued that a special fund with its own permanent institutional setting should be established, but the finance ministry resisted the idea and this forced the government to create a separate committee to examine this question. Nore, who was also a member of this committee, says the Ministry of Finance succeeded in torpedoing the idea. 'We lost the fight,' he says.

Economic historian Einar Lie says that memos written by Ministry of Finance officials at this time showed they resisted the fund because they had little faith in the ability of the political class to exercise restraint; they feared that a 'popular variant, a fund that would invest in infrastructure and Norwegian industry, would win acceptance'.[193] In effect, they foresaw the creation of a second funding mechanism that would rival the national budget and become another source of government spending. The dramatic rise of Statoil as a financial force in the economy, given its ability to distribute contracts to businesses around the country, seemed to echo these concerns. And prominent Labour Party figures, most notably the former industry minister Finn Lied, made a strong case for domestic investment in nation-building projects. Lied made this argument in an influential lecture called 'Norway's foreign exchange reserves – passive investment or growth stimulus for the nation'.[194] The paper reinforced the view within the Ministry of Finance that the fund would become a readily available source of capital that could be used to finance measures through channels not controlled under the standard budgetary process. One memo from the economic policy department to the secretary-general and finance minister foreshadowed a new era of furious rent seeking by various interest groups in the event of creating such a fund: 'An oil fund … would seem deeply attractive to groups that consider themselves unfairly treated in the prioritization of the government budget. All so-called non-inflationary expenditure proposals would see the oil fund as an alternative source of funding to the standard budget.'[195]

This concern was underscored when a parliamentary report from the Ministry of Petroleum and Energy argued in favour of using oil revenue to boost Norwegian infrastructure, growth capacity and industrial expansion abroad. Subsequently, Finance's economic policy department set up a ministerial committee with a mandate to set up a fund, but the majority report returned with a recommendation for a fund that was in reality a standard government deposit account at the central bank. In response, Finance moved to block the creation of a new fund even though a senior adviser to conservative prime minister Kåre Willoch was strongly in favour of the Skånland concept.

As the oil boom gained momentum during the 1980s, an economic bubble grew progressively larger. It was fuelled by the rapid loosening of credit controls and expansionary government spending, which was in part consistent with the aim spelled out in the 1974 white paper of using oil revenue to create a 'qualitatively better society'. Emboldened by the oil revenue that was being collected and then immediately spent, both conservative and Labour governments embarked on widespread financial liberalisation while at the same time keeping interest rates artificially low, thereby creating the pre-conditions for a financial bubble. This was in sharp contrast to the practices followed for most of the postwar period, when Norway had operated a tightly controlled financial sector that used rationing of credit to keep domestic demand in check.[196]

This regulatory system, though archaic, had created what Knutsen and Lie called 'a stable framework for banking', which resulted in negligible losses on loans. However, in an oil-fuelled economic boom, cracks emerged in the system as banks began finding ways to deviate from these interest rate controls and meet the increased demand for credit. When the global economy began a full upswing in 1983 following the early 1980s recession, banks were able to 'evade and circumvent' the credit regulations, and a credit boom prevailed. In the space of a few years, the Oslo Stock Exchange had quadrupled in value and real estate prices doubled in the four years to 1987. The country became caught up in the euphoria of an oil-fuelled asset price bubble. 'Swift price increases of collateral paved the way for an increase in credit, which in turn triggered off a further rise in asset values,' as Knutsen and Lie noted.[197]

The expansion was driven by two of the country's biggest banks, which fuelled credit growth peaking at 30 per cent per quarter in 1986. Norway's biggest bank, Den norske Creditbank (DnC), increased its total assets fourfold between 1980 and 1986. Its employee numbers increased by a third and the number of branches outside Oslo increased from 75 to 136, reflecting the drive by regional offices to write bigger and bigger loans. The boom also inspired offshore expansion, with the bank acquiring fully owned subsidiaries in New York, London, Singapore and Hong Kong. A second bank, Christiana Bank (CBK), also embarked on an aggressive expansion strategy. In 1980 it acquired Norway's fourth-largest bank and increased its assets over the next six years by a factor of six, making it the second-largest bank in the country. At the peak of the boom, the two banks controlled more than half of the country's financial assets. Both banks encouraged clients to borrow as much as they could, and new forms of marketing fuelled the lending, including the transferring of loan-writing authority to car dealers, while Norwegians began hosting 'home parties', where guests were able to obtain personal and home loans.

The party couldn't last forever, and the inevitable downturn was precipitated by an oil-price slump in 1986, when prices almost halved and plumbed a low of $12 a barrel. It had the effect of taking the punch bowl away from the party, as it delivered a decisive hit to national income and growth. It highlighted the vulnerability of Norway's newly acquired prosperity, and its dependency on oil prices to underpin its standard of living. In order to boost corporate profitability, the government cut the special tax rate on oil production from 35 to 30 per cent, and announced that royalties would not be applied to new fields. Oil revenue plunged from 35 billion kroner ($4 billion) in 1985 to just 6 billion kroner ($920,000) in 1988.

The Norwegian economy went into a deep recession. The Conservative government proposed a radical austerity program but was unable to secure parliamentary support for it, leading to its dismissal. In May 1986, a Labour government won office led by Gro Harlem Brundtland, who became prime minister for the second time. As the banking crisis unfolded, Norway found itself in serious economic trouble. The central bank tried to rescue the economy through devaluation but this failed to prevent a deep recession taking hold again in 1989 and lasting for two years. The recession triggered spiralling loan losses for all of Norway's banks, especially DnC and CBK, which in turn led to a run on the banks and government intervention to rescue them. CBK experienced a run in 1991 and deposits continued to slump until the government stepped in and 'clarified beyond doubt' that it would guarantee the bank's solvency.[198] Other smaller banks experienced runs at around the same time. In spite of this, the main feature of this crisis was not a contagious banking panic driven by depositors scrambling for high-powered money, but rather a solvency crisis, caused by widespread credit losses.

This bitter experience, more than anything else, was the catalyst for the political class and the bureaucrats to finally set up a petroleum fund. Brundtland's government lost parliamentary support in 1989 and was replaced by the Conservative Party. The new finance minister, Arne Skauge, called for the creation of a petroleum fund, without giving any direction on how it should be designed.[199]

The bureaucrats in his department set about drafting a new bill 'with little enthusiasm'. The head of the ministry's economic department, Svein Gjedrem, who went on to become central bank governor a decade letter, wrote in a memo at the time that the political signals were 'so clear that there is no avoiding it'.[200] As economic advisers searched for ideas of how to create the fund, they were aware of the experience of Alaska, which set up the Alaska Permanent Fund in 1976, and the Canadian state of Alberta, which set up the Heritage Savings Trust Fund in the same year. Former finance minister Kristin Halvorsen has said that Norway was 'inspired' by the Alberta model, but that fund has been plundered by politicians over the years and to this day has assets of only C$17 billion.[201] The Alaskan fund was created by a constitutional amendment which stipulates that 25 per cent of all oil-related revenue is deposited into it, and it then pays out dividends to bona fide Alaskan citizens. Economist Martin Skancke, who was working in the Ministry of Finance at the time, says the Alaskan model was seen as flawed. Says Skancke: 'I cannot recall us looking in detail at any other fund. We tried to develop this more from first principles. I think we felt from a macro point of view that Alaska was inappropriate, where the fund distributes cash to the citizens and then is forced to raise more tax revenue. That seemed inefficient and inappropriate.'[202]

Alaska has at the very least done better than the Canadians, given that the market value of the fund in January 2016 was $49 billion. The capital has continued to grow even though oil production has been declining steadily. On a per capita basis, the Alaskan fund is worth around $255,000 for each of the 192,284 citizens, which is slightly more than Norway's, at about $180,000 per capita. Alaska's dividend payments remain a reasonable $2000 per annum.

Taking stock of their misgivings from earlier in the decade, Norway's finance ministry officials wrote into the bill a series of checks and balances designed to avoid the populist outcomes they had feared. They based the operation of the fund around three key principles, all of which remain in place today. The central bank governor Øystein Olsen, who was working in the finance ministry at the time, describes the fund's design as 'technically a simple construction', but indeed this is one that has stood the test of time. First, all revenue from petroleum activities notionally bypasses the budget and goes directly into the fund. However, in practice, the fund would appear to work quite differently to this principle because of the way it is integrated into the budget. Even though all of the oil revenue is allocated to the fund, the government then draws down to finance its deficit, so the transfers to the fund in the early period especially would be equivalent to the government's budget surplus. Skancke, who headed the asset management department in the Ministry of Finance from 2006 to 2011, says there was no point having a fund showing assets if the government was simultaneously accumulating massive deficits, so the budget and the fund had to be integrated:

> The fund mechanism entails that money will only be allocated to the fund when there is a budget surplus. This reflects an important point: running a budget surplus is the only way a government can accumulate financial assets on a net basis. If a fund is set up with an allocation rule that is not linked to actual surpluses, the accumulation of assets in the fund will not reflect actual savings.[203]

The second principle puts all of the fund capital into foreign currency, thereby taking it out of the domestic economy and putting some downward pressure on the Norwegian krone. This has proved to be fundamental to the success of the fund. Not only does it avoid creating a bubble during good times, it creates a natural hedge against lower oil prices, which can be used to boost the economy. It also means that the fund is able to invest in foreign assets at relatively lower prices during the boom years, when the krone is stronger. And during times of lower oil prices, when the krone is weaker, these assets can be cashed in and returned to the budget for a much greater return in local currency. As such, this design principle makes the fund a veritable cash cow. The third principle is that all spending of the fund's return must be approved by parliament as part of the budget process.

As Einar Lie points out, these design features were the result of 'Norway's own hard-won experience' in the first decades of oil development. The spending binge of the '70s and '80s influenced the budget integration. But Norway's own poor record in managing an income insurance scheme established in 1967 strongly influenced the decision to invest all of the assets in foreign currency. What's now known as the Government Pension Fund Norway suffered from excessive political influence, which meant that it was forced to lend at sub-commercial rates, and so its returns suffered.[204]

The politicians and advisers who created the fund did not think that much capital would ever be transferred into it, given the parlous state of Norway's finances at the time. 'There was no master plan to have an account with the size it is today,' says Olsen. And even when the budget was balanced, the community's expectations regarding the use of oil revenue meant that most of the increased revenue would likely be spent, just as was in the 1970s. 'Experience over the previous 15 years had also indicated that Norway had been in a position to spend large amounts of oil revenue domestically, even though the macroeconomic consequences had been unfavourable,' wrote Lie.[205] Despite this pessimism, left-wing Norway, with its emphasis on discussion, debate and long-term planning, was certainly doing much better than so many other resource-rich countries.

While Norway clearly struggled during the 1970s and '80s, the contrast with the UK over the same period is stark. Unable to capitalise on the opportunities presented by its new-found oil wealth, the country's imploding industrial base led to rising unemployment and a financial bailout. Between 1970 and 1976, the unemployment rate doubled to reach 6 per cent, or 1.3 million people. It more than doubled again to reach a record 13 per cent by 1982, or 3 million people.[206] Mounting budget deficits and a collapse in the sterling forced the Labour government to call on the International Monetary Fund to provide a $3.9 billion facility in 1976, which according to Britain's National Archive was 'the largest amount ever requested of the Fund'. The IMF had to secure additional funds from the

United States and Germany in order to provide the facility.[207] Given that the rise in oil production coincided with surging unemployment to a record level, it's fair to say that most of the UK's North Sea oil revenue was spent on unemployment benefits.[208] This neo-liberal approach could not be more different from what Norway has achieved. Its state-led approach meant that windfall oil revenue was first invested directly in the North Sea, through both Statoil and the state direct financial interest, and then from 1990s onwards this money was used to build the world's biggest future fund.

7

TROLLING THE SOVIETS

'Countries participating in the agreement will not commit to
any incremental deliveries of Soviet gas ... and participate
in the accelerated development of alternative Western energy
resources, principally Norwegian gas reserves.'

US National Security Decision Directive 66,
signed by President Ronald Reagan, 1982

A VISITOR TO DOWNTOWN OSLO IN THE MID-1970S MIGHT
have thought that a space invader had landed. Right there in
the middle of the harbour, and visible from the centre of
town, a giant steel hulk was emerging from the waterline. Norway's
oldest shipping company, Aker, had invented a new type of semi-
submersible drilling rig for the rough conditions of the North Sea,
which it was building in the centre of Oslo. It was abundantly clear
to all that the country's firm approach with Big Oil was already
paying dividends.

As a correspondent from Britain's *The Economist* magazine
observed during a visit to Oslo at the time, Norwegian entrepreneurs
had 'moved into the offshore oil industry with breathtaking speed'
and they had developed new technology that was already being
exported around the world.[209] The Norwegians were in fact showing
far greater entrepreneurial flair than their British counterparts and

had broken the monopoly of American companies in oil rig construction, securing a 20 per cent market share in the space of just a few years. 'It is a record to shame every British shipbuilder,' *The Economist*'s correspondent wrote.

The rig observed by the correspondent was called an H-3, a platform designed so that drilling operations could continue in bracing conditions, thereby substantially reducing the downtime that oil companies experienced on the North Sea. This made the search for oil far more economical than it had been in the past. Despite being an old-establishment company, Aker had indeed been very quick to respond to the new opportunities presented by the North Sea and the government's helpful push. In 1966, just one year after Norway launched its first licensing round, Aker had built the *Ocean Viking* drilling rig, which went on to discover the Ekofisk field. Norwegian companies were building a fleet of 150 supply ships to service the growing number of platforms in the North Sea. The country's ability to industrialise and add value to its primary production indicated that it was already building a post-oil future. As *The Economist* noted in a very prescient comment: 'It is a guarantee that Norway will be making money out of oil long after the flow from the North Sea has dried up.'

Despite these successes, Americans companies still had a tight grip on this industry, as nearly all of the equipment that went onto these platforms was American-made, and so were many of the people who worked on them. In trying to break into this new industry, the Norwegians both invented new technology and adapted existing practices to the North Sea. Most importantly of all, as *The Economist* noted, they were very quick at taking an idea and turning it into a saleable product.

The technology used by Norway to conquer the North Sea would eventually be developed on a breathtaking scale. But this technology wasn't only for the purpose of developing oil and gas. In the case of the biggest development of all, the Troll gas field, its four concrete towers would be used against the gas-rich Soviet Union in a bid to bring down Communism. Not only was Norway building a new industry, this committed member of the Western Alliance was also doing its bit to fight the Cold War. Jens Christian Hauge, who had ushered Norway into NATO as defence minister and then inspired its oil-based industrialisation, would have been very proud to see politics and industrial strategy work so cohesively.

Norway's ability to leap into this new industry seems even more incredible when compared to the natural and acquired advantages that Britain had at the time. The Second World War had been the catalyst for the UK to develop many of the building blocks for this new industry. The Mulberry Harbour built for the D-Day landing showed how Britain could harness the best engineering capacity in a time of war, but a generation later it failed to apply its skill and technology to oil extraction. Former civil servant Norman Smith points out that British engineer Guy Anson Maunsell designed floating rigs to support anti-aircraft batteries in the River Thames during the war. These platforms were virtual prototypes of the rigs used decades later in the North Sea. And, he adds, the country's engineers developed flexible pipelines to supply petroleum to the Allied armies as they advanced into France in 1944, which was the same technology later applied to the oil industry. These developments came about because of the 'close links between government and industry which existed during the war', says Smith, but such imperatives didn't apply in peacetime. 'The British invented these things and then forgot about them,' he says.[210]

In a belated effort to help its struggling engineering industry, the UK government set up the Offshore Supply Office in the mid-1970s, at around the time *The Economist* visited Oslo. Smith, who had financed North Sea projects for Barings Brothers for a decade, headed this office from 1977 to 1980. Smith says one key factor in

Norway's success was that its companies didn't try to reinvent the wheel: 'Norway had no subsea production experience. They adapted things that had been developed in the Middle East. In the 1980s, the UK was miles ahead in subsea technology. They had developed it back in 1975. The Norwegians used the UK as a hunting ground for skills and technology,' he explains. The proactive approach of Statoil and Norsk Hydro, working together with local engineering firms, made the country a world leader in subsea production systems and multiphase technology. These technologies involved putting much of the hardware on the seabed, rather than above the waterline, which enabled the Norwegians to safely produce petroleum in very rough conditions. Multiphase technology involved moving multiple types of hydrocarbons over long distances, allowing remote resources to be exploited in a way that had never been done before. Smith adds, 'The Norwegians were able to take a concept and drive it through to a product,' often in a very short space of time.

While Norwegian business initially knew next to nothing about the oil industry, the country's long history as a shipping nation proved to be an effective springboard for this new opportunity. It wasn't just technical skills. A key factor in this initial take-off was the financing system that had been developed around the shipping industry, according to historian Gunnar Nerheim.[211] Den norske Creditbank estimated in the mid-1970s that Norwegian entrepreneurs were investing around $10 billion in building infrastructure – drilling rigs, production platforms and supply ships – for the oil industry over the next five years.[212]

Norway's shipbuilding empires were ideally located and staffed to take advantage of this new industry. Almost every major coastal town in Norway had a major shipyard, with both skilled workers and engineers. But Statoil's Arve Johnsen wasn't convinced that these dynasties would be able to adapt to the demands of this new industry so he decided that Norway needed a new organisation to compete effectively. He applied the same philosophy as with the creation of Statoil, and together with Finn Lied and Jens Christian Hauge, he 'forced' Aker and Kværner to create a new entity, to be known as Norwegian Petroleum Contractors (NPC). The company was founded in 1977 just as construction work for three mammoth new fields – Frigg, Gullfaks and Statfjord – was gearing up.

Each of these projects would push the boundaries of technology due to the sheer size of the oil and gas installations. Statfjord alone would involve three giant platforms made of concrete and steel. The engineering companies were able to draw on the experience of Norway's hydro industry in using reinforced concrete to build dam walls. As this industry had expanded in the 1950s and 1960s, many skilled engineers were on hand. Norway was also able to take advantage of its geography as its deep fjords were ideally suited for building enormous structures, which were then towed out to sea with numerous tugboats. When Phillips was building the storage tanks for the Ekofisk facility, it opted for concrete in order to satisfy the demand for local content. After building the concrete break-water and tank, the century-old engineering firm Høyer-Ellefsen set about building more of these concrete islands with a new design called Condeep (short for concrete deep water structure).[213] The design involved building a hexagonal base comprised of numerous cells which was often about the size of two football fields. This base, known as a gravity base system, would sit on the seabed to support concrete towers reaching up hundreds of metres to the water's surface. The first Condeep went into British waters for a field called Beryl, followed by the remote Frigg field in 1976. Straddling the maritime boundary between the UK and Norway, 190 kilometres west of Bergen, the Frigg gas field involved construction of three concrete structures from 1976 onwards – one for drilling and production, and two for gas processing. The Condeep design wasn't entirely original because the first concrete platform for Frigg was a French design built in Scotland. But the Norwegians quickly moved in and they built the remaining two structures. Construction of the drilling and production platform was won by NPC, giving the new company its first big contract. This involved building a massive concrete breakwater that was a similar design to the one at Ekofisk. The following year, the same shipyard at Åndalsnes produced a Condeep structure for the second gas-processing plant.[214]

From this time onwards, shipyards along the west coast of Norway between Stavanger and Bergen began turning out more of these concrete giants, each one larger than its predecessors, and each one pushing the boundaries of science and technology. As energy analyst Daniel Yergin put it, the engineering effort required to develop the North Sea's resources in the 1970s and 1980s became 'one of the greatest investment projects that the world had ever seen'.[215] In all, fourteen Condeeps were built in Norway between 1975 and 1995, each of them located in deeper water and consequently involving much bigger and heavier concrete foundations and taller shafts (see Appendix C). The first Statfjord platform to be built, known simply as A, was built by a joint venture between the American engineering giant Brown & Root and Norway's Aker. The joint venture came about after Aker vigorously lobbied the government and Statoil for a piece of the action. The American industrial giants simply had to accept a role for a Norwegian business.

When Mobil looked to build the second Statfjord production platform, known as B, the company convinced Arve Johnsen that giving Aker a prime position wasn't in the country's interest. So Kværner, Norway's second-largest engineering firm, was awarded the project management role. Aker then had to downsize the massive yard it had built outside Stavanger. Both Aker and Kværner each had one main yard outside Stavanger where the platforms could be assembled, with smaller yards to produce modules that were later added to the main structure. Engineering works were booming around Oslo as well, and in Kristiansand further south. The numbers of engineers employed by these firms tells the story of just successful Norway was at both generating skilled engineers and capturing business. In 1974, about 10 per cent of Kværner's 6558 employees were engineers. By 1988, its workforce had grown to 9744 employees and more than one in five was an engineer. This increase was in step with rising local content, from around 20–30 per cent before 1975 to more than 60–70 per cent with the development of the Statfjord platforms. From 1984, the Ministry of Petroleum and Energy ceased publishing these figures because Norway was doing so well, it feared that the government would be accused of engaging in protectionism.[216]

Norway's protectionist approach had clearly proved effective in building up enormous engineering capacity, but this was not a policy that could be sustained indefinitely. The beginning of the end for the local content policy arrived in the early 1990s when Norway and other members of European Free Trade Association (EFTA) joined the EU common market, even though they did not become members of the European Union.[217] Norway had co-founded the EFTA with Switzerland in 1960 and then in 1994 it joined the European Economic Area, an internal market governed by the EU trading rules. With the stroke of a pen, all of Norway's supportive programs for local content, technology, jobs and onshore development were swept away. Norway could no longer insist that foreign companies set up local subsidiaries; all that was needed was company registration in Europe. Workers from any European country could be employed in the Norwegian industry, and Norway could not make it a proviso that oil and gas be landed onshore. The royal decree of 1972, which had set up the protectionist regime, was abolished. These changes took effect on 1 January 1994, twenty-five years after the discovery of the Ekofisk field. But instead of seeing the Norwegian industry smashed by a flood of foreign competition, the changes became a catalyst for the industry to go global with a 'Team Norway' approach. Norwegian companies were encouraged to work together to compete internationally, selling their technology and expertise to the world.

Michael Porter's 1990 book, *The Competitive Advantage of Nations*, became an influential blueprint for how the country could go about building up clusters of innovative businesses, according to historian Helge Ryggvik. Instead of competing against each other, cooperation became king. This led the Labour government to launch in 1993 the trade agency INTSOK, which stands for internationalisation (INT) of the Norwegian Continental Shelf (SOK). Set up by Jens Stoltenberg, a future prime minister who served as petroleum minister at the time, INTSOK was tasked with encouraging companies to reduce costs by working together and becoming more competitive. This 'Team Norway' approach resulted in a fivefold increase in revenue during the 1990s, and by the 2000s the oil service industry became the second-biggest earner of export revenue after oil and gas.

Even though the protectionist policies that underpinned the Condeep structures were the very antithesis of the capitalist ethos, they certainly proved invaluable when the United States wanted to develop Norwegian gas resources to undermine the economy of the Soviet Union. This strategy culminated in building a Condeep comprising four towers that would be higher than the tallest building in the US, towing them 70 kilometres from the coast and planting them in a water depth of 300 metres. For a country with a population of around 4 million people at the time, this was an engineering feat on a monumental scale.

WEAPONS OF ECONOMIC DESTRUCTION

When the US government learned at the height of the Cold War that Norway had discovered one of the world's biggest gas fields, its national security advisers saw the potential to use this find as a weapon against the Soviet Union. The field, which became known as Troll after the mythological giant, produced copious amounts of gas when it was first drilled in 1979, the same year the Soviets invaded Afghanistan.

In Norway's fourth licensing round in 1978, the Dutch giant Shell won the rights to explore a block that was well known to geologists though it was considered marginal and located in water depth of more than 300 metres. Chevron had previously dismissed the potential of the geological 'flat spot' when it reviewed seismic data in the early 1970s. Shell was unfazed and immediately commissioned the drilling rig *Borgny Dolphin* to drill exploration wells in the area. The results proved encouraging. On 5 September the Norwegian Petroleum Directorate issued a press statement declaring that 'a gas field with substantial reserves' had been found. The announcement quickly generated great interest, and it wasn't just within the oil industry.[218]

Notwithstanding the excitement, bringing Troll to life would involve many years of technology and infrastructure development. The shallow reservoirs made it what one geologist called 'the biggest marginal field in the world', so geologists would have to find a way to tap the resource that would make the project economical.

The Soviet Union was also a very big gas producer and it was looking to prop up its struggling economy with gas sales to Europe. In fact, the only part of the Soviet economy that seemed to be growing was gas exports.[219] This was the late 1970s and the Soviet Union was beset by slowing economic growth, falling living standards, crumbling health care and rising military spending driven by the invasion of Afghanistan. Even oil production was falling. With this context, the massive size of the Troll field, more than the combined resources of Ekofisk and Statfjord, meant that it grew in importance to US national security advisers. Even though

Shell didn't declare the field commercial until 1983, shortly after its discovery was made known US foreign policy planners began working on using Troll as a Trojan horse to help bring down the Soviet Union. William Martin, secretary of the National Security Council, conceived the idea of promoting Norwegian gas to replace supplies from the USSR. Western European countries were negotiating with the Soviets to buy as much as 40 billion cubic metres of gas, and the US was concerned about European dependence on Soviet gas and the revenue that this would deliver to the Communist country. The US had imposed trade sanctions on companies involved in building a 3700-kilometre Siberian gas pipeline designed to supply gas to Europe. Reagan proposed that sanctions would be lifted in return for a European agreement not to purchase any more gas from the Soviet Union.

At a meeting of the Group of Seven major nations in 1981, Reagan urged US allies to find alternative sources of gas. Joined in Ottawa by German chancellor Helmut Schmidt, British prime minister Margaret Thatcher and French president François Mitterrand, among others, Reagan said the West's energy strategy should be seen as a key part of the Western Alliance's foreign policy. The following year Reagan signed US National Security Decision Directive Number 66, which called on Allies to get behind the development of Norwegian gas resources. The directive outlined the 'security-minded principles' that would govern East–West economic relations 'for the remainder of the decade and beyond'. The first principle related to the preference for Western European countries to buy gas from Norway:

> ... countries participating in the agreement will not commit to
> any incremental deliveries of Soviet gas beyond the amounts con-
> tracted for from the first strand of the Siberian pipeline; not
> commit themselves to significant incremental deliveries through

(handwritten margin note: Instead of soviet sources, so that the soviets couldn't gain revenue during cold war)

already existing pipeline capacity; and participate in the accelerated development of alternative Western energy resources,
principally Norwegian gas reserves.[220]

Having elevated development of Norwegian gas resources to the
very top of US foreign policy priorities, the Americans then wanted
Norway to rush Troll into production. This approach reflected little
understanding about the mammoth scale of the work involved to
develop a field in 300 metres of ferocious water. During 1982, the
year in which Reagan signed the directive, the US government
began applying serious pressure to Norway to bring Troll onstream.
With its work coordinated between the departments of state and
energy, the US government summoned the Norwegians to Washington to discuss how they could achieve this result. The
Norwegians didn't appear to take the pressure too seriously as they
sent a delegation headed by Hans Henrik Ramm, the junior minister for petroleum and energy. The cigar-smoking Ramm and his
team explained how it was still early days in the development of
Troll. The discovery had not yet been declared commercial by Shell,
and the field extended into neighbouring blocks awarded to other
companies that had not yet been opened for exploration.[221] Ramm
explained the complex nature of the field: how it was located in
deep water with shallow reservoirs, which would require complex
technology and many drainage points, and how its development
would involve laying pipelines across the very deep Norwegian
trench. The American side didn't really understand Ramm's argument, and they asked whether it would help if the US government
put more pressure on American oil companies to speed up development. Finally, Ramm made his point by picking up bottles of
mineral water and stacking them on top of each other as he
explained that Troll would require building concrete towers and
platforms that would stand 471 metres tall from the seabed to the

heliport, each around 90 metres taller than the Empire State Building. 'We've got to build an Empire State Building, and then another, and then another, and that's when Troll will be ready,' explained Ramm, omitting to mention in his haste that in fact a fourth tower would be needed.[222] The Americans fell silent.

The US officials seemed not to understand the long-term nature of the gas supply, which would work in favour of the objectives that US foreign policy was seeking to achieve. Any gas development relied on negotiating and then signing supply contracts that were decades long, so it didn't matter if actual delivery was a decade or more away – what mattered was that the Norwegians would be able to sign gas contracts that would deny future revenue to the Soviet Union. The prospect of major gas supplies coming from Norway allowed Reagan to achieve his objective of freezing the sales of additional Siberian gas to European nations. Reagan had been so successful that by the end of 1982, he announced that the trade embargo on companies involved in the Siberian pipeline was no longer necessary. While he didn't specifically mention Norwegian gas when announcing an end to the sanctions, Reagan said in November that year that the sanctions would be lifted because 'we've achieved an agreement with our allies which provides for stronger and more effective measures'.[223] Shell declared the Troll field commercially viable the following year, but it took another three years for the consortium to finalise the gas contracts that would underpin the development.

Another thorny issue to contend with, however, was that development needed to find a way to extract the thin layer of oil that lay beneath Troll's gas. A more measured approach to developing Troll would allow geologists to extract as much of the oil as possible; this was clearly in Norway's national interest, though it was not in the interests of the US government or Shell, as it happened. When Shell submitted plans in the early 1980s it also hoped to bring the Troll gas field onstream as quickly as possible.[224] The proposal paid little regard to the oil because Shell believed that its production would be unprofitable. Shell and the US government might have had their way if not for the influence of Iraqi geologist Farouk Al-Kasim, who became the man of the moment when he took on the might of Shell and the US government over the development of Troll.

One of the most enduring memories of Al-Kasim's upbringing in the Iraqi port city of Basra were the flares that lit the night sky. These flares epitomise the wasteful practices in oil and gas extraction and processing, but even so, Al-Kasim became fascinated by the industry that burgeoned around his home town. He had worked his way up through the ranks of the newly created oil administration, and became director of resource management in the NPD. He quickly realised that the challenge with Troll was to find a way to extract both the oil and the gas, and that a rushed development could leave behind most, if not all, of the oil. Exactly that had happened just a few years earlier when the Frigg field went into production as a gas-only operation. Frigg, like Troll, contained a thin layer of oil measuring about seven to fourteen metres in thickness.[225] These strata made Frigg a substantial oilfield but extracting it would have required the drilling of several hundred production wells, which at the time was entirely uneconomic.

Extending over a vast area of 700 square kilometres, Troll's gas and oil resources were divided into three distinct zones, each with very different characteristics. Extraction of the resources would require three separate facilities. Troll had two separate oil provinces of about 14–26 metres in thickness. In all, the field had recoverable reserves estimated at 1330 billion cubic metres of gas, making Troll by far Norway's largest hydrocarbon find. In oil-equivalent terms, Troll amounted to more than 11 billion barrels of oil. The gas resources alone would supply all of the gas consumed today by Australia and the United Kingdom combined for 130 years.[226]

Al-Kasim realised that a project of this scale needed a cross-disciplinary team to analyse the discovery and ensure Shell was going to develop the field in a way that maximised the benefit to the people of Norway. He appointed reservoir engineer Ole Svein Krakstad to lead the group, and as numbers grew they took up offices in a former carpet shop on the ground floor of the NPD's then head office in Stavanger. Al-Kasim gave Krakstad free rein to recruit the experts he needed to analyse the entire production process, including specialists in geophysics and economics.

The massive size of Troll meant that it extended beyond Shell's licence area and into neighbouring blocks controlled by Norwegian companies: Statoil, Norsk Hydro and the privately owned Saga. When the NPD asked all four companies to submit development plans in June 1984, Shell gave no weight at all to oil extraction, and it maintained that gas production itself would be barely profitable. Al-Kasim's Troll team disagreed, noting that Shell had not considered the use of horizontal drilling.[227] None of the four operators saw any prospect of using horizontal drilling, largely because they believed that these very long wells could cause the reservoir to de-pressurise. Another concern was that the additional time needed to develop this technology would delay gas sales. In fact, the Soviet Union had drilled horizontal wells as far back as the 1930s, and by the 1980s the country had drilled many such wells, mainly under ice caps, but they weren't sharing their know-how with the West.

Aside from the technical arguments, the Norwegian government faced the prospect of each of the four individual companies acting independently and thereby undermining the overall level of production. The government soon realised that it needed to unitise the four licence areas to make sure the companies acted together. Even though there was no law in place that enabled the government to make such a directive, the NPD relied on little-known 'provisional regulations for acceptable exploitation of petroleum resources' to order the companies to unitise the field. And to ensure that companies took a long-term view and avoided rushing to exploit the resource, the NPD extended the duration of the unitised licence to 2030, adding an additional fifteen to nineteen years to the original terms.

While Shell remained adamant that horizontal wells were too risky, especially given the water depths, the Troll team at the NPD pressed Norsk Hydro in 1987 to drill two virtually horizontal wells in the oil-bearing strata on what became known as Oseberg South. The NPD also came up with a plan to reinject the gas from Troll to increase the recovery of oil. It even invented a new name for the technique, TOGI (Troll Oseberg gas injection). This technique would not only boost oil recovery, it would also trial a 'multiphase' flow of oil, water and gas over long distances, which Norwegian companies had been at the forefront of developing. Resistance to horizontal wells was broken when Gro Harlem Bruntland won office in the mid-1980s. Arne Øien, the economic adviser who had told the foreign companies how they would pay a super-profits tax a decade earlier, became the new petroleum minister, and it was Øien who now told Statoil that it had to get behind the TOGI concept. Øien admonished Statoil when he chose to award the operator role for the oil-producing part of Troll to its arch-rival, Norsk Hydro.

Unitisation laid the basis for a three-phase development, starting with the gas in Troll East, then the oil in Troll West and finally the Troll West gas. Al-Kasim's determination resulted in Norway's extracting 1.5 billion barrels of oil from Troll, adding a conservative $50 billion in revenue to the coffers of the Norwegian treasury, or more than 5 per cent of the value of the petroleum fund.

A STATE WITHIN A STATE

At the time of the Troll discovery there were growing concerns among conservative politicians in Norway about the rising power and influence of Statoil, and the company's central position in developing this immense resource served to demonstrate its supremely powerful role just one decade after its creation. Initially, Statoil had a 50 per cent interest in the block where the main discovery was made, known as 31/2. Even though Shell was the operator of the project, its stake was only 35 per cent.[228] But after Shell declared a significant find in 31/2, the Labour government awarded neighbouring blocks to Statoil, Norsk Hydro and Saga. When these other blocks were unitised, Statoil's interest rose to a commanding 85 per cent. What's more, the licence awarded to Shell stipulated that Statoil could take control of the field ten years after it was declared commercial, which meant 1993.[229]

Statoil was given this privileged position when the Labour government was in office and the policy of giving preference to state-owned companies was at the forefront of the government's strategy to maximise benefits to Norway. Statoil's Arve Johnsen had argued in favour of the company securing 100 per cent of Troll. While many countries around the world were relying heavily on foreign capital to develop their oil and mineral resources, Norway was putting in place policies to ensure that its resources were developed with Norwegian capital so that the profits would remain at home. At that time, Norwegian equity interests controlled only about 20 per cent of petroleum production in the country, largely because Phillips and other multinationals controlled the prolific Ekofisk field. But this strategy meant that Norway was on track to lift that share to more than 60 per cent by the end of the 1990s, when Troll came onstream.

The conservatives came into office in October 1981 with a mandate to reduce Statoil's dominance, and over the next five years the new government set about doing that. As the company had strong support from within the Labour ranks, this policy created a great deal of political heat, but the conservatives prevailed. The new prime minister, economist Kåre Willoch, described Statoil's dominance as dangerous for Norwegian society because the company was destined to become more powerful than the government. The conservatives believed that Arve Johnsen was buying political support for his company through the awarding of contracts to Norwegian businesses.[230] Willoch believed that Statoil was more powerful than the Ministry of Finance:

> The place gained by Statoil in operations on the Norwegian continental shelf represented nothing less than an invitation to waste. Secondly, the company had a management that was willing to use any means to gain political influence. That made Statoil a state within the state.[231]

Willoch feared that Statoil was managing too many big projects at the one time, and he questioned the merits of the company moving into downstream operations like refineries and even retail distribution. It was at this time that Statoil embarked on building a huge and costly refinery at Mongstad, which culminated in the axing of the entire Statoil board, and Johnsen's role as chief executive, in 1988. Willoch's fears were confirmed two years later when Statoil was found to have influenced a contract that benefited a business owned by employees. While the Norwegian civil service had remained corruption-free, the same couldn't be said for the national oil company. When a lucrative maintenance contract for the Statfjord platforms was awarded to the Norwegian company Seaway, competitors complained that they had offered lower rates. It soon emerged that one of Seaway's ships, the *Seaway Pelican*, was in fact owned by the twenty-seven Statoil employees under a limited company structure. A Statoil inquiry found that the tender process had set parameters that were designed to suit the ship.[232]

One of the key reforms introduced by Willoch's government was to strip Statoil of its control of the state's equity interest in oil and gas fields. This interest was renamed the state direct financial interest (SDFI), to be controlled directly by the government. This decision reduced Statoil's interest in Troll to 30.58 per cent, with the SDFI controlling 56 per cent. In 2001, the SDFI was transferred to a new entity known as Petoro. Johnsen contends that Willoch's agenda was purely political, and it overlooks the rise of Statoil as a global player in the industry, which is something that no other Norwegian oil business has achieved: 'The conservative government would curb Statoil under any circumstance. From the very beginning this was their main policy in the 1970s and 1980s. My opinion has alway been that nothing succeeds like success. The two other Norwegian petroleum companies from the 1970s – Saga and Norsk Hydro – never stood the test of long-term endurance and global competitiveness.'[233] Today, Statoil remains 67 per cent owned by the Norwegian state and is one of the world's top twenty oil companies. It's even gone into business with the Russians. In 2014, the Statoil chief executive Helge Lund signed a joint venture agreement in the presence of President Vladimir Putin to explore the Arctic region.[234]

LAST GIANT

Developing a field that covered an area of 700 square kilometres would require the building of three enormous platforms that could withstand the conditions of the North Sea for more than half a century. The biggest of them, known simply as _Troll A_, with its four concrete legs, would turn out to be taller than the tallest building in the world at the time. The job of designing and building _Troll A_ was won by NPC, the group set up by Arve Johnsen in a bid to get more local content into the industry. NPC had also built the concrete legs for the Statfjord platforms, but this project would require engineering on a much grander scale. *Troll A* would become the biggest job undertaken by this firm, and indeed the last big concrete structure built in the North Sea. Its concrete base and towers were comprised of nineteen cells and four shafts that were braced about halfway up to stiffen the towers for the tow out to sea.[235] In all, the completed structure weighed 1.3 million tonnes, making it the largest man-made structure ever moved on the planet. Concrete 'skirts' built underneath the cells were designed to penetrate thirty-six metres into the seabed, giving the structure additional stability. The 360-metre-tall towers required 245,000 cubic metres of concrete and 100,000 tonnes of reinforced steel. When completed, the concrete towers alone were thirty metres taller that the Sears Tower in Chicago, which at the time was the world's tallest building, but the height rose for another 112 metres when the steel structures were built on top. The total height, from the base to the top of the flare stack, was 472 metres. Construction, which took four years and a peak workforce of 2000 people, began in 1991 in dry dock near Stavanger before the entire structure was towed north to the city of Vats where the steel infrastructure was craned on top.

When towed into position, pipelines extended out to forty production wells drilled more than 1000 metres into the seabed, each with a capacity of processing 3.4 billion cubic metres of gas per day. The platform collected the gas and pumped it 68 kilometres to an onshore processing plant located at Kollsnes. The development had gone ahead even though building the pipeline was going to be another high-risk operation. When the parliament approved the development, the approval was contingent upon the NPD vouching for the ability to conduct diving down to 300 metres. But by the time the build got underway, undersea robots were used to do most of the construction work.[236]

The New York Times carried a story on its front page when the massive structure was towed out to sea by ten tugboats, generating 130,000 horsepower. They moved it at a rate of one–two knots an hour, depending on the weather.[237] At one point, near Kvitsøy Island, it cleared the seabed by a mere ten metres. *The Times* noted in passing that the value of the gas contracts in place until 2022 was $100 billion and that no less than 85 per cent of the revenue from these sales would be returned to the Norwegian state. Even though Troll had been used to defeat Communism, this massive revenue haul could also be seen as a triumph for Norway's socialist approach to oil development.

The gigantic Troll A *platform being towed out to sea in 1995.*
Image courtesy of the Norwegian Petroleum Museum.

When pictures emerged of the dramatic tow-out, a former energy adviser in the Norwegian embassy in Washington sent copies to William Martin, the former secretary of the National Security

Committee. Martin ensured that President Ronald Reagan received one of the photos as well. While Reagan was in the final years of his life at the time, Martin reminded him that his sanctions on Soviet pipelines to the West and emphasis on developing Norwegian gas was one of his greatest foreign policy achievements. This was, Martin wrote, 'one of the major contributors to the rapid decline of the former Soviet Union'.[238] Even though Arve Johnsen had left behind his career at Statoil by the time Troll went into production, he could take pride in his belief that the development of Troll, and the strategically significant role that it played in European geopolitics, ranked alongside Norway's contribution to winning the Second World War.[239]

8

CASH COW

'It is likely that future generations will hold the view that we could have saved even more.'

Svein Gjedrem, architect of the Petroleum Fund law, 2010

FIVE YEARS AFTER NORWAY'S PARLIAMENT PASSED THE Government Petroleum Fund law, the government's finances and the economy were in such a parlous state that the fund still showed a zero balance. This was a sad reflection of the consequences of boom and bust in a country that had been well aware of the risks of a resource bonanza, thus demonstrating the difficulties faced by all resource-dependent nations. But in 1995, as oil prices recovered and production soared, Norway's new Labour government, led by the first female PM, Gro Harlem Brundtland, recorded a small budget surplus. In May the following year it deposited a sum of 1.981 billion kroner ($314 million) into the Petroleum Fund (it was renamed the Government Pension Fund Global in 2006).[240] This was a modest start, and it was a small fraction of the 70 billion kroner ($11 billion) in gross oil income generated that year. On 31 December 1996, the Ministry of Finance transferred a second deposit into the fund, this time a much more substantial 40 billion kroner ($6.15 billion). The government created a new account with the central bank, in addition to the one that it already had, and the surplus was transferred directly into this account and then invested into foreign currency bonds. In the beginning, all of the funds were invested safely in risk-free government bonds.

The timing of these first two deposits coincided with a significant turning point in Norway's success as an oil nation. After the disappointments of the late 1980s, two key policies introduced two decades earlier finally began to pay massive dividends. First, from 1995 onwards, the twenty-year-old special tax began collecting more revenue than ordinary company tax. In that year, revenue from the special tax exceeded company tax collections by around 30 per cent, and it has continued to exceed ordinary company tax in every year since.[241] The gap between the special and ordinary taxes has continued to widen, averaging about 70 per cent over the past fifteen years. But even more significant was the revenue from the government's direct investment in oilfields, known as the state direct financial interest (SDFI). In the late 1990s, SDFI generated more revenue than the company and special taxes combined, and over the past decade it has raised as much or more revenue than the special tax. Two decades earlier, no-one envisaged that Norway would ever collect so much revenue from its petroleum production, but this revenue haul shows the benefit of putting in place sound policies in the event of a commodity boom.

Norges Bank officials weren't expecting the fund to become operational, so the central bank hadn't created any of the structures or management systems when these deposits were made. In the first two years of operation, the central bank invested these monies in the same way as it managed foreign exchange reserves. In 1997, the Ministry of Finance transferred an even more substantial 64 billion kroner (around $9.5 billion) into the fund, or about three-quarters of oil revenue generated that year, thereby lifting the total savings to more than 100 billion kroner ($14 billion) within two years, and the following year it began making quarterly transfers into the fund.

The initial deposits triggered a debate within the government on how to manage the fund savings. Various options emerged, such as creating a new institution, but Norges Bank became the obvious candidate even though this was seen as problematic. One of the factors against Norges Bank was that, should it run into problems as a fund manager, this would also reflect on its primary role as manager of the money supply, thereby potentially undermining confidence in the entire economy.[242] One faction within the central bank advised its governor, Kjell Storvik, not to accept the role.[243] On the other hand, the _Petroleum Fund Act_ said that the funds should be invested in the same way as the country's other assets, which were also managed by Norges Bank. Storvik decided that Norges Bank should take on the role of fund manager, so he began setting up a separate unit within the bank.

Martin Skancke, a senior official in the Ministry of Finance at this time, recalls that the debate shifted in favour of giving the role to Norges Bank because its strong independence and existing governance safeguards meant it could defend the fund against the much-feared political opportunists who might want to interfere with its operational management and indeed raid the nest egg. 'The perceived risk was that a new institution would be more difficult to shield from inappropriate intervention. The central bank had a good governance system, an independent board. The bank had a strong reputation and the feeling was that that could support legitimisation of the fund,' he explains.[244]

Both the Ministry of Finance and the bank began working on creating the capacity to manage the billions of dollars as they came rolling in. Governor Storvik looked outside the bank to recruit new staff. One of the key recruits was Knut Kjær, who had worked in the private sector for the past two decades after a brief stint in academia and as a researcher at the central bank. Kjær had topped his year when he completed a master's in economics in the early 1980s, which he researched at the central bank. He then spent a few years at the University of Oslo before deciding that the private sector was more his calling. He'd been raised in a family of typically Norwegian entrepreneurs. Just four years after leaving university, Kjær joined together with three other colleagues to set up an economic analysis business, ECON, which they built into a significant company. Kjær left in 1994 to become executive vice president of Storebrand, a large financial firm, before being recruited by the central bank. Kjær says that as well as being known to the senior officials in the bank, his business experience meant 'they knew they would get something different'. They wanted a results-driven organisation rather than a public-sector behemoth. 'It was a case of being there at the right time. Of course, it was the opportunity of a lifetime,' says Kjær. He was just forty-one when in spring 1997 he joined the bank as a special adviser to set up the investment arm, and the following year he became the first executive director of what became known as Norges Bank Investment Management (NBIM).

The following year Kjær was joined by Svein Gjedrem, appointed governor of Norges Bank for a six-year term. Gjedrem had already played a pivotal role in drafting the petroleum fund law. Another foundation recruit was Yngve Slyngstad, who had a strong background in economics as well as private-sector experience with Storebrand as its Asian equities manager. Slyngstad, thirty-six at the time, was made chief of equities. Kjær regards Gjedrem as a 'key' individual to the creation of the fund. Not only did he oversee the drafting of the fund law, Gjedrem also developed the governance framework for NBIM's operation, which was put into regulations approved by parliament in May 1997. Norway could have taken a passive approach and simply invested in indices and tracked the market, but instead it opted for a strategy aimed at achieving 'the highest possible return subject to the limits set out in the Regulation', while also ensuring that risk-management systems and controls were in place.[245] The regulations also set out a transparent approach for assessing the performance of the fund.

Gjedrem, who was forty-five at the time he became governor, was a career bureaucrat in the Ministry of Finance when he developed the fund law in the late 1980s. He was a Stavanger local who had attended the prestigious Cathedral School, where he proved to be a good sportsman. He played first-division football for the Vikings and Lyn teams in his home town before graduating in political economy. His strong suit was mathematics, and this led him into roles with the central bank and the Ministry of Finance.[246] Gjedrem exemplified Norway's long line of pure, principled bureaucrats, and would continue the tradition and indeed build on the foundations established by Hermod Skånland and Per Schreiner in their landmark reports. He was promoted to permanent secretary of the ministry in 1996, followed two years later by his appointment as governor, where he suddenly found himself in the limelight.

After his first year as governor, Gjedrem admitted that it hadn't been smooth sailing for the central bank as it set up the systems to safely manage the country's future wealth, including a move beyond government bonds and into equity markets around the world. As he wrote in unusually frank language in the fund's first annual report:

> During the past two years, Norges Bank has faced considerable challenges in connection with the preparation and implementation of the new management strategy for the Petroleum Fund, and this task has received high priority. The Fund is a very important economic policy instrument, and shall promote the long-term considerations pertaining to the use of petroleum revenues. Broad confidence in the manner in which this important part of our common financial wealth is managed is therefore

important. Clearly defined roles and responsibilities, and openness about management results, are preconditions for confidence
in the management of the Fund.[247]

By the end of 1998, NBIM had a staff of about seventy as it prepared
to deal with more substantial deposits. When NBIM produced its
first annual report in 1999, the accumulated capital had grown to
172 billion kroner ($22 billion). NBIM purchased its first equities
just three weeks after it was created, and by the end of 1998 the
fund had permission to invest in equity markets in twenty-one
countries.[248] From 1999 onwards, NBIM moved into more active
management of its assets, which it achieved through both internal
operations and by appointing fund managers. It outsourced the
active management of its Japanese assets.[249] However, at the same
time NBIM was developing its own capacity to engage in active
trading and from early 1999 onwards it engaged in in-house trading of its equity portfolio.[250]

The government needed to find a way to assess the performance
of NBIM's investing and to this end a system of benchmarking was
introduced by the Ministry of Finance. The system, which is standard practice in funds management, created a virtual portfolio for
equity and bond investments. Known as benchmark portfolios,
NBIM's performance is measured against each of these benchmarks. But the fund is prevented from taking excessive risk as the
governance arrangements imposed by the Ministry of Finance fix
an upper limit to how far NBIM may deviate from the benchmark
portfolio. The Norwegians were confident from the outset that the
approach they were taking would allow them to beat the market,
and the record shows that they have done so, though not significantly. In the first decade of the fund's operation it did reasonably
well, outperforming the benchmark by 0.39 per cent, although this
margin has since come down to 0.26 percentage points, the NBIM

chief executive Yngve Slyngstad told a parliamentary committee in 2016.[251] Slyngstad was appointed chief executive in 2008 after Kjær decided to return to the private sector. Even though NBIM claims to operate along private-sector lines, its salaries are a fraction of those paid in the investment banks that manage much smaller portfolios. In 2015, Slyngstad's took home less than $800,000, although the equities chief Petter Johnsen earned around $1 million. These salaries might explain why NBIM launched a campaign against inflated executive salaries.

Former finance ministry adviser Martin Skancke, who now advises countries around the world on setting up sovereign wealth funds, says the performance of Norway's fund has been 'good but not spectacular', and this is because of the risk limits imposed by the Ministry of Finance: 'The limits are very, very small, and so the fund is really invested close to the indices. There is very little active management. In a statistical sense the returns are not very different from zero.'

Asked to respond to this point, Slyngstad says: 'Our task is to safeguard and build financial wealth on behalf of future generations. The overall return has been 26 basis points higher than the return on the benchmark indices since inception. However, the absolute return on the fund over time will to a large extent be determined by developments in the broad markets the fund is invested in.'[252] But Skancke's point begs the question: why doesn't NBIM simply invest directly in a portfolio comprised of this index, thereby eliminating the need for investment managers? Kjær argues that the index approach is more suited to small investors and it would be been more costly for NBIM to have adopted this model. From a finance theory viewpoint, the composition of the index is constantly changing, which makes it costly to maintain a portfolio that is exactly the same as the index. He says: 'There are many pitfalls with index management. For retail investors they are a good thing.

For a large investor, there are inefficiencies from how the index definition is created as prices are changing every day.'[253] Skancke says that one model Norway could look to is the New Zealand Superannuation Fund, which has been 'incredibly successful', though he notes that Norway's fund is now so big that such an approach may be problematic: if the managers chose to deviate from the benchmarks and target certain stocks or sectors, this could artificially inflate the price of these investments and in turn defeat the goal of diversification. 'The Norwegian approach has been very conservative, just because of the size of the fund you are constrained to invest in line with the broad market indices,' he adds.

Despite this low-risk strategy, the inflow into the fund, combined with the investment performance, have reaped a phenomenal revenue flow over the past decade. The fund increased its assets seven-fold in the decade to 2015 (see Figure 1) to a peak of about around $930 billion in the first quarter of 2015. Just under half of this massive capital base was the result of transfers from the government into the fund, while returns on investment amounted to about one-third of the capital. And just slightly less than one-fifth was the result of favourable currency fluctuations, which underpins the strategy of investing in foreign currency. But in recent times, the rise in the US dollar from mid-2015 onwards, and weakening oil prices, brought the value back to $870 billion by June 2016. Even at this reduced level, the fund is the largest sovereign wealth fund in the world (although China and the US have multiple funds that when combined exceed this value). Volatility on global markets have proved to be a huge opportunity for the way this fund works, given that it uses a rebalancing instrument that virtually operates as a money spinner on autopilot. When global equities plunge, and the value of the fund's holdings fall as a share of the total value, the fund managers automatically know that they should be acquiring more equities. The opposite applies when markets surge and the share of equities in the overall portfolio increases well beyond 60 per cent. The rebalancing of the fund during the global financial crisis in 2008 proved to be a huge opportunity to buy into blue chip equities at bargain basement prices, which in 2009 led to its best-ever annual return of 26 per cent. The fund began moving into equity markets in emerging countries from 2000 onwards, and into real estate from 2010 onwards.

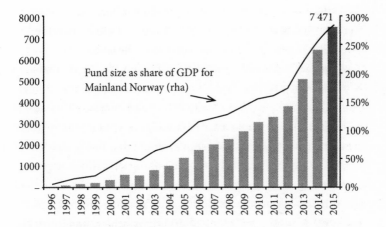

Figure 1. Value of the Government Pension Fund shown in billions of kroner and as a share of non-oil GDP. The US dollar value peaked at $930 billion in Q1 of 2015 before ending the year at around $860 billion as the US dollar rallied.

In the first quarter of 2016, just under 60 per cent of the fund assets were invested in equity markets around the world, while bonds accounted for 37 per cent of assets and real estate for 3 per cent. Its capital now accounts for close to 1.5 per cent of global equities. In regional terms, the fund invested just under 40 per cent of its assets in Europe, and the same for the United States, but in recent years the share devoted to Asia has grown to 15 per cent, reflecting a new emphasis on emerging businesses. Nestlé was the fund's single biggest investment, worth more than $6 billion. Its top investments look very twenty-first century, with three drug and personal care companies (Novartis, Roche and Johnson & Johnson), three IT businesses (Apple, Alphabet [Google] and Microsoft), two financiers (HSBC and Blackrock), and two oil companies (Shell and Exxon).[254] The Norwegian parliament has declared that coal companies are no longer acceptable, prompting the fund to dump fifty-two of them in early 2016, but about 6 per cent of the fund's assets remains invested in oil and gas businesses.

The switch to real estate, which began in 2008 following a decision by the Ministry of Finance, involves holding a maximum of 5 per cent of the assets in property. NBIM's plan is to 'build a global, but concentrated, real estate portfolio', which means focusing on some of the world's major cities: London, Paris, New York, Washington, Boston and San Francisco. In coming years the fund is looking to move outside Europe and the United States, 'primarily in Asia'. Some of the recent acquisitions sound like a game of Monopoly. So far, the returns have been very good. In the 2015 year, the fund earned a real return of 10 per cent, although after this strong result the value dipped in the March quarter of 2016 by 1.3 per cent.

PERVERSE EFFECT

As is often the case in dealing with resource abundance, the petroleum fund policy had the effect of allowing the Norwegian state to both save and spend at unprecedented rates. Previously, the government had put in place a physical brake on Norway's oil development – the policy introduced as part of the 'go slow' strategy in the early 1970s that limited annual production to 90 million tonnes of oil per annum. The creation of the fund meant that the country could develop its resources as fast as was physically possible, because it now had a financial mechanism to moderate the economic impact of the revenue derived.

Norway surpassed the production limit of 90 million tonnes in 1989, the year before the law to create the fund was introduced, and production continued to ramp up throughout the 1990s before reaching a peak of 221 million tonnes of oil in 2004, almost 2.5 times the original limit.[255] The merits of Norway's new policy framework meant that the country could have its cake and eat it – up to a point. The reality was that Norway was dealing with a finite resource that had reached its peak level within thirty-three years of production having commenced, so perhaps even more restraint was called for.

Removing the physical constraint meant that Norway became even more dependent on developing its petroleum resources to underpin its high standard of living, and its generous welfare. Norway, like any Western democracy, was dealing with demands to spend more, and these pressures became acute from 2000 onwards when the rising oil prices and production – especially after Troll came onstream – led to a tsunami of revenue, which in turn made the capital in the fund grow strongly. In 2000, Norway's total oil revenue more than tripled to 222 billion kroner ($25 billion), followed by another sharp rise in 2001 to 325 billion kroner ($36 billion). Both sides of politics strongly supported more extensive spending while keeping the policy of saving for future generations. Prime Minister Jens Stoltenberg introduced a new spending rule. Øystein Olsen was working in the Ministry of Finance at the time when politicians looked for a policy to increase spending in a way that could be regarded as sustainable. He says it became clear that Norway was in effect running a neutral fiscal policy, which meant that over the course of the economic cycle, all of the oil revenue would in fact be saved: 'The understanding around professionals was that this is not wise or possible to never spend anything. So there was time for change. We relatively quickly came out with this present fiscal rule which says that oil revenues should be spent over time but in a very controlled way. We should save for future generations but oil spending should match the real return on the capital.'[256]

As Gjedrem said at the time in his capacity as central bank governor, the government and the parliament had agreed to new 'guidelines' for managing petroleum revenue that would allow spending 'equivalent to the expected real return on the Government Petroleum Fund', which was set at 4 per cent. This new policy amounted to an increase in the use of petroleum revenues of about 0.4 per cent of mainland (non-oil) GDP each year up to 2010, which was a very substantial rise.[257] Gjedrem noted that the policy had strong support across the political spectrum: 'A clear majority in the Parliament supported the Government's long-term strategy for using petroleum revenues.'

The central banker defended the increased spending to economic conservatives on the grounds that the new rule would provide a steady means of introducing oil revenue into the domestic economy, thus avoiding the boom–bust approach of the 1970s and 1980s. While the bureaucrats had allowed fiscal policy to be more expansionary, it coupled this action with an inflation target of 2.5 per cent to make monetary policy a more effective tool in restraining demand. From Gjedrem's perspective, the two policies were closely linked.

> If budget outlays are allowed to swing in pace with oil prices, the result may be abrupt shifts and instability in the Norwegian economy. The Government was of the view that a clearer anchor was required to reinforce monetary policy's role in underpinning stable economic developments. This is why Norges Bank was given a new operational mandate for monetary policy.[258]

The result of this new policy was a rapid increase in spending from 2001 onwards. Even though the economy was doing well, annual spending grew at more than 3 per cent in real terms by the mid-2000s, the fastest rate since the recession of the early 1990s. This expansion was in fact driven by a centre-right government led by the Christian Democrats, which introduced budgets in every year from 2001 to 2005 that greatly exceeded the 4 per cent limit. Martin Skancke, who was director general at the prime minister's office at the time, says that exceeding the limit in part reflected the sharp drop in returns that followed the dot com crash. But nonetheless, the amount of spending measured in krone did rise sharply. The first budget introduced by this new government in 2002 more than doubled the budget deficit to around 60 billion ($7.5 billion), and it continued rising over the next three years.

Jens Stoltenberg returned Labour to government in 2006 and did some serious budget repair, but spending blew out again beyond the 4 per cent limit in 2009 and 2010 as a result of the global financial crisis. At this time, the structural deficit had increased to more than 100 billion kroner ($18 billion). After the GFC, spending was reined in for one year only, 2011, and then it has increased by more than 2 per cent in every year since. But the size of the fund doubled in the four years to 2015, allowing the Norwegians to spend increasingly larger krone amounts of their giant nest egg, while remaining well within the 4 per cent spending limit.

Even though Gjedrem had implicitly approved of the spending increases by not publicly criticising it, he lamented some of the largesse in his final year as governor. In a 2010 speech he noted that increases in oil spending could not go on, especially given the fact that production and revenue were declining while the demands of the welfare state, and the ageing population, were steadily rising. He went as far as saying that it was too early to determine whether Norway had been a sound manager of its oil endowment, and that future generations may harshly judge the spending by present-day Norwegians. In an address to the University of Oslo, Gjedrem said:

> Even though sound institutions have been built for the management of Norway's oil wealth, it is too early to assess the effectiveness of our management. And even though the pressure to spend even more oil revenues has been considerable, it is likely that future generations will hold the view that we could have saved even more.[259]

The driving force behind these questionable levels of government spending in Norway are the extensive welfare benefits combined with high levels of public-sector employment, both in direct government jobs and state enterprises. Hilde Singsaas, who was deputy minister for finance in the former Labour government, praises the way Norwegians leave work from 4pm onwards. 'Many people, especially women, work part-time. On average we don't work a lot, but productivity is high. Most Norwegians go home to their families in the afternoon about 4–5pm. That is the Norwegian way of living – we want people to combine working life and their family obligations,' she explains.[260] The generous welfare system clearly delivers some benefits to the country, which has one of the highest rates of female workforce participation in the world. This in part reflects the policy of offering twelve months' paid parental leave with universal access to childcare at highly subsidised rates.

Singsaas says a key part of the strategy to lift female participation has been the mass expansion of childcare centres. 'We manage to combine a high fertility rate and high employment among women, mainly due to the family policies of government since the 1990s. In the 1970s, there were not many kindergartens and the majority of women were housewives. We have now what we call total coverage. You have the right to access the kindergarten from the age of one and at the same time we have parental leave for one year. This is a doubling since the end of the 1980s. So this has been a high priority for the Norwegian politicians so that women can combine family obligations with working life.' Mother of three Liv Nordhaug attributes her ability to juggle work and raising three children in Oslo to the factors outlined by Singsaas. 'The combination of the long maternity leave and the guaranteed admission to a kindergarten has been crucial for us deciding to have three children,' Nordhaug says.[261] 'If these arrangements hadn't been in place – or had been significantly less generous – I think we would have stopped at two.' In between having each child, Nordhaug has been able to juggle flexible work with her employer, Norad, the country's development agency, and her husband took advantage of paternity leave for three months.

Others say the benefits make Norway more innovative. Anyone starting a business knows they can fall back on the state if they fail. Any worker who loses their job can enjoy a pension of 80 per cent of their previous salary for up to two years. But given these benefits, it's no wonder that a new verb – to 'nav' – has emerged in Norway, relating to one's ability to extract benefits from the state.[262] One in three workers in Norway works in the public sector, compared with one in five in the OECD. Three-day weekends are common and disability benefits are rising sharply. Norway spends almost 6 per cent of GDP on disability and sickness benefits, the highest of any OECD country and almost three times the OECD average of around 2 per cent.[263]

Defenders of the spending rule can point to the fund's return to justify the policy. The key variable in this new policy was the expected rate of return on the petroleum fund. Over the life of the fund, the real return had averaged 3.9 per cent, so the 4 per cent rule appears to be appropriate, at least in hindsight, though the limit may be too high given the outlook for returns and oil revenue in the future.

Despite the rise in oil prices to more than $100 a barrel from 2012 onwards, the central bank has been trying to convince politicians to lower that spending limit. In 2012, Governor Olsen used his annual speech to call on the then Labour government to reduce the spending rate to 3 per cent. He argued that a more restrained approach was required because, in a post-GFC world, interest rates were likely to remain lower for a considerable period and returns on the fund were likely to be commensurately lower. In his second address to the supervisory council of the central bank, Olsen said:

> The real return on bonds in the fund's portfolio can now be estimated at 1 per cent. With a normal risk premium on equities, the real return on the whole fund can be quantified at 3 per cent. In the expectation that the current low interest rate environment will prevail for another 10 years, we think it will be difficult to reach 4 per cent given our present risk profile.[264]

Prime Minister Stoltenberg said in response that Olsen could be setting a dangerous precedent. For example, if fund returns increased at some point in the future to 5 or 6 per cent, then the new policy could trigger demands to increase the rate of spending accordingly.[265] Olsen agreed that the argument had some merit, in that 'you should not end up with fiscal policy following actual return'. However, given the outlook for future returns, Olsen says that conservatism is called for: '[It is] better to be on the lower side.'[266] Kjær says there's fairly compelling evidence to indicate that returns are likely to be lower in the future and this calls for a more restrained approach to spending. 'It is always a question about balance. On a year by year basis, what is sustainable, that is a balance you can never calculate just the right number. The policy can be seen as generous for future generations because you don't touch the asset. Four per cent has been a sustainable return in the capital.'[267] Asked if 3 per cent would be more prudent, he agrees, and notes that a recent white paper on spending oil revenue forecast returns closer to 3 per cent over the next ten to fifteen years. However, data for the past 120 years shows that for a balanced portfolio, 4 per cent real return has been the average: even though there have been periods of ten years or more when the return was negative, there have also been periods when returns have far exceeded this very long-run average.

A year later, with the oil price haven fallen from more than $100 a barrel to around $50 a barrel in the space of a few months, Olsen reminded politicians that the fund would reach its peak level far earlier than expected, and therefore there was now an even greater need for restraint:

> At today's oil price, the GPFG may have reached the peak. In that case, petroleum revenue spending as a percentage of GDP must be reduced to avoid using more than the return on the GPFG. Even if the oil price and the rate of return follow a path that allows the GPFG to grow for a period ahead, petroleum revenue spending should be restrained.[268]

PROGRESS AND POPULISM

One of the main reasons why Norway has been less restrained over the past fifteen years is the rise of political populism and opportunism, which appears to be linked to the country's increased wealth. Populism in Norway is mainly embodied in the Progress Party, which has consistently campaigned for sharp cuts to immigration, the deportation of illegal immigrants and breaking the golden rule of investing all of the fund's assets abroad.

Formed in 1973 as a party of protest against Norway's high taxes and government intervention, the Progress Party achieved its best election result in the 2013 national poll when it secured 16 per cent of the vote and forty-one seats, making it the second-largest party in parliament. It then formed a coalition government with the conservative party, and secured six influential cabinet positions, including finance, transport and communications, and petroleum. Progress's taking of the finance portfolio involved dumping the long-serving finance spokesperson. So far, Progress hasn't been able to achieve the domestic investment of Norway's assets, but it has certainly achieved even higher levels of spending despite the decline in oil revenue.

Ketil Solvik-Olsen, forty-three, one of the Progress Party's young up-and-comers, gives some assurance that the party's rise won't lead to a raid on Norway's wealth. At first, he comes across as a neo-con heavily influenced by the time he spent studying in the United States. He did a high school year as an exchange student in Michigan before studying economics and political science at the University of Toledo, Ohio. The American influence can be seen in his parliament house office, which is adorned with models of very big American cars, mostly Chryslers, part of a collection of more than eighty. He also owns a couple of real American classics, a Cadillac and a Dodge convertible.

Solvik-Olsen, who became minister for transport and communications in 2013, says that in Norway he is considered 'extreme right' but in fact his views line up with the Grand Old Party. His greatest hero is Ronald Reagan. Incredibly, even though Progress is a low-tax party, Solvik-Olsen and his peers still firmly believe that the country's very high taxation on petroleum is sound policy and not something that should be changed. However, he advocates a more flexible approach with lower tax for marginal fields: 'We all agree pretty much that natural resources like minerals, oil and gas, and water for hydropower are common goods. Thus it is accepted that these resources may have high taxation to make sure the "windfall profits" go back to society. Oil and gas are so profitable that you accept a higher tax rate – at 78 per cent. I don't think we should lower tax on oil companies much from today's level. But for certain fields with more marginal resources, you should be able to discuss the tax rate. It is better for government to have 60 per cent of something than 78 per cent of nothing.'[269]

In other words, with the higher rate of tax, some oil developments won't go ahead, so it's better to see these marginal fields go into production at a lower tax rate than have nothing at all. However, Solvik-Olsen agrees that the 78 per cent tax rate on oil comes with some very favourable depreciation that enables companies to write off investments in just six years, compared with eighteen years for other industries. But it's on investment of the fund assets that Progress harks back to the fears raised by the Ministry of Finance in the 1980s when they believed that a 'popular variant' would emerge. Solvik-Olsen argues that the golden rule of investing exclusively off-shore should be changed for domestic projects that are deemed to be of national significance. The argument is appealing, and popular for some. He says:

> The spending rule, which forces us to save most of the government income from the oil industry, is a good thing. However, our budget system does not distinguish between investment and consumption, so any extra oil money spent in the domestic economy is treated as regular consumption. That is where we want to change it. We want to make a distinction and move certain capital objects out of the budget and into dedicated government-owned companies. If you see improved road infrastructure as a means to boost growth rates and GDP, then we should invest some more of the oil income into a government road company. Now we see the oil fund buying foreign bonds with low yield, while domestic infrastructure projects lack funding.

So far, despite the Progress Party's influence, these ideas have yet to be embraced by the centre-right government. What's more, the party's standing in the community may be on the wane, though it's not because of its populist stand on oil revenue. The anti-immigration party suffered its worst result in twenty-two years at the 2015 local elections. The party's vote slipped below 10 per cent, well down on the 16 per cent that it polled in the 2013 national elections.

The revised 2016 budget deficit delivered by the finance minister, Siv Jensen, also a member of the Progress Party, expanded the deficit to 206 billion kroner ($25 billion), equivalent to 2.8 per cent of the value of the fund. While this appears to look responsible, given that it is below the lower limit proposed by Olsen, it may prove to be unsustainable in a new era of lower returns on the fund. As Olsen pointed out in an address in December 2015, about one-third of the fund's assets were invested in bonds, and the return on them was heading to zero.[270] This was why the fund was now looking to invest more of its assets in real estate, most likely at the expense of the bond portfolio. But the contrast with the last oil price crash in the mid-1980s is indeed stark. As Olsen said in his 2016 annual lecture, the country could be headed for a very long 'winter', but it is now eminently better equipped to deal with it: 'The Norwegian economy has enjoyed an exceptionally long summer. Winter is coming. The Norwegian economy is well equipped to tackle the challenges. The defence mechanisms of economic policy are better suited today than when oil prices fell in the mid-1980s. At that time, current oil revenues were largely spent over the government budget. When oil prices plummeted, the budget was severely tightened.'[271]

Should the oil price remain at recent modest levels, the merits of the policy approach of the past twenty years will be self-evident, given the large amounts of wealth that were stored away during a two-year period of above $100-a-barrel oil prices. Equally, it shows that the rate of spending needs to come down if this policy is to remain sustainable into the future. In this new era, Olsen warns that

Norway will have to begin eating into the stored wealth within the fund. 'We are approaching the point where government spending of petroleum revenues will exceed the revenues deriving from the petroleum sector. At today's oil prices, transfers to the GPFG will soon fall towards zero,'[272] said Olsen, at a time when the oil price was around $40 a barrel.

THE ACTIVIST INVESTOR

Five years after the first deposit went into the fund, the amount of capital accumulated had started to grow substantially and was worth around $50 billion. This was a miniscule amount when compared with the value today, but even so at this early stage the Norwegians realised that they could do more with their money than make more money. In 2000, a new Labour government led by the youthful Jens Stoltenberg, who was forty when he became prime minister, created a sub-portfolio within the petroleum fund known as the environmental fund. This formally came into being on 31 January 2001 with an initial deposit of 1 billion kroner ($111 million).[273] The environmental fund had a brief to invest in companies that met specific environmental requirements, or were deemed to have a limited negative effect on the environment. The investments were based on analysis from the British consulting firm Ethical Investment Research Service. The initial endowment was doubled the following year.

Ethical concerns about how Norway was investing its capital then led the Ministry of Finance to examine whether investments in the main portfolio should be excluded for ethical reasons. It created an Advisory Commission on International Law for the petroleum fund. The commission was not autonomous, but at the request of the Ministry of Finance it was tasked to assess whether specific investments were in conflict with Norway's commitments under international law. Five months later, the government chose to dump shares in Singapore Technologies Engineering because it was 'considered highly probable' that the company was engaged in the manufacture of landmines.[274]

This first exclusion led to the development of a systematic policy for excluding companies for a range of ethical concerns. In late 2004, the Ministry of Finance issued ethical guidelines for the petroleum fund that contained a so-called exclusionary mechanism, and the Advisory Commission on International Law was replaced by the new Advisory Council on Ethics, tasked with reporting on a regular basis about ethical issues associated with the fund's investments. At about the same time, the environmental fund was subsumed into the main portfolio. The fund's value was almost $200 million, making it a sizeable portfolio that could project significant financial and political clout in global markets. From 2005 onwards, the fund began excluding companies that produced cluster bombs (Raytheon and General Dynamics Corporation) and nuclear arms (Honeywell, Airbus and Boeing). From 2006 onwards, NBIM began divesting from businesses that engaged in 'serious or systematic human rights violations', including the US retail giant Walmart, for its labour practices, and those that caused severe environmental damage, including Rio Tinto in 2008. A comprehensive ban on companies engaged in tobacco manufacturing was then introduced in 2009, which went on to affect twenty-one companies including the maker of matches Swedish Match. More recently, NBIM has added 'gross corruption', 'other particularly serious violations of fundamental ethical norms', and 'serious violations of the rights of individuals in situations of war or conflict' to its list of eight criteria for banning companies. In all, NBIM has now excluded sixty-five companies (see Appendix D).

Even though Norway's wealth derives directly from petroleum, the country has now taken a stand against fossil fuel companies, and the pressure to do this has mainly come from parliamentarians. Hans

Olav Syversen, a lawyer who chairs Parliament's Standing Committee on Finance and Economic Affairs, says MPs have been debating the issue of fossil fuel investment for a number of years, and that his party, the Christian Democrats, together with the Liberals, came up with the policy in the first instance.[275] Once these two parties joined together, Labour came on board. He explains that the policy reflected concern about both environmental and financial risk: 'My party wanted a broader approach: Is it a vice to both produce oil and gas and reinvest in oil and gas companies – to put all eggs in one basket? Unfortunately the government and majority in parliament left that issue early on and no agreement came into place regarding the financial risk question.'

Following a request from parliament to examine this issue, the Ministry of Finance appointed an expert group in April 2014 to assess the fund's investment in these companies. The committee was chaired by Martin Skancke and included several professors and technical experts. Its report recommended against automatic exclusion of fossil fuel businesses: 'In our view, fossil fuel companies' energy production, energy use or CO_2 emissions cannot per se be said to be contrary to generally accepted ethical norms.' Instead, it recommended that Norway observe and exclude these businesses on a 'case-by-case basis'. It explained that companies could be excluded 'where there is an unacceptable risk that the company contributes to or is responsible for acts or omissions that, on an aggregate company level, are severely harmful to the climate'.[276] It recommended that the application of this criterion be left to the Council on Ethics, essentially a business-as-usual approach.

Following this report, the finance ministry amended the management mandate for the GPFG and the guidelines for exclusion and observation to differentiate between product-based and conduct-based criteria. The amendments came into effect on 1 January 2015.[277] However, pressure from parliament to go even further remained, so the finance minister, Siv Jensen, outlined a new policy in April 2015. She said the government agreed with the findings of the expert committee and would 'introduce a new criterion to exclude companies whose conduct to an unacceptable degree entail greenhouse gas emissions'.[278] Jensen said the new criterion was 'broad in scope, and not limited to specific sectors or types of greenhouse gases'. In addition, she noted that active ownership and engagement by the fund remained a powerful tool that could influence action on climate change. The fund had in recent years made more than 100 risk-based divestments, including holdings in coal extraction and coal power companies. The ministry would also ask Norges Bank to conduct a specific risk-based review of portfolio companies whose involvement in coal extraction, coal power generation or coal-based energy conversion represented a significant part of their business.

While this statement was a significant advance, parliament maintained pressure to specify a threshold for divestment. In May, it made a unanimous decision to ban the fund from investing in coal and power utilities that derived more than 30 per cent of their income from the mining or burning of coal. A parliamentary statement said emphatically: 'All the parties in the Storting have reached agreement that the GPFG will no longer invest in coal companies. The Government has now been requested to invite Norges Bank and the Council on Ethics for guidance in preparing the criteria for the withdrawal.'[279]

Given the strength of this statement, it was highly significant that when Norges Bank and NBIM responded to Jensen's request for a policy review, they took into account the specifics outlined by the parliamentarians' statement. An August 2015 letter to the Ministry of Finance signed by the governor Olsen and NBIM chief executive Yngve Slyngstad spells out a new policy regime that accords with the parliament's ban on investments in companies earning more than 30 per cent of their income from thermal coal, while excluding coking coal, which is used to make steel. Olsen and Slyngstad said the new criterion would affect investments in around 120 companies with a market value of more than $7 billion. The transaction costs involved in divesting these stocks would amount to around $50 million. In April 2016, NBIM's first round of analysis led to the divestment from fifty-two coal companies, most of them in the United States and China. The response by these two top economic advisers shows how parliament is still very much in the driving seat of developing oil policy, as has been the case since the very beginning. Slyngstad said that in a democracy this is entirely appropriate:

> If you run a sovereign wealth fund in a democracy and there are limits to what the population want to make money on, those limits have to be put up by the political establishment that is representative of the population. It is a reflection of the Norwegian population's sentiments and instincts with regard to where we want to make money for our grandchildren.'[280]

Norway's decision to act on coal companies may seem like a double standard given that it omitted the original remit of coal and petroleum. Nevertheless, it certainly sent a shudder through the stock market valuations of these companies at a time when they were being battered by a freefalling coal price. This clearly shows the benefit of the direct investment approach. As well as delivering somewhat higher returns to present and future generations of Norwegians, it has also given immeasurable influence to this small country. As NBIM argues, this approach allows the fund to 'exercise all our ownership rights', and indeed this is what NBIM has done through active engagement with the companies it owns share in, and by fully exercising participatory rights as a shareholder. This strategy has culminated in a phenomenal amount of engagement and influence for Norway. In 2015 alone, NBIM attended more than 11,500 shareholder meetings and held 3520 meetings with senior executives to discuss their operations in detail (this was almost 1000 more than in the previous year).[281] NBIM argues that its active shareholder engagement will ultimately 'benefit the people of Norway'.

In addition to ethical investment, NBIM has now gone further by adding what it calls the principles of 'responsible investment', which it began outlining from 2008 onwards as part of so-called expectation documents.[282] Action on climate change was one of the key criteria. Commencing in 2014, NBIM began publishing an annual 'responsible investment' report tracking corporate behaviour in relation to children's rights, water management, climate change and human rights. The report goes as far as tracking the carbon emissions of more than 9000 companies in the investment portfolio – 4.3 million tonnes of CO_2 equivalent in 2015 or 128 tonnes per million dollars.[283] Based on poor compliance in these areas, NBIM divested from seventy-three companies in 2015 alone. The ethical and activist dimension to the GPFG demonstrates to the world that it is possible to not only accumulate massive wealth, but to do so in a way that helps to make the world a better place.

*

After a decade-long boom followed by a precipitous slump in oil prices throughout 2015 and into 2016, some might think that Norway has relied too heavily on oil and that it's now found itself in a very tight corner. From an economic perspective this is true, but the financial strength of the country will certainly carry it through these tough times. Not only did Norway maintain strong economic growth and near full employment in the years after the global financial crisis, it has no net debt whatsoever, while net state assets alone amounted to $850 billion at the end of 2014.[284] This position was in stark contrast to where Norway found itself in the late 1970s, when it had per capita income in line with Greece and struggled to manage its new-found wealth. In 1978, net foreign ownership of Norway's financial assets amounted to 41 per cent of GDP, but over three decades this position has now been completely transformed to the point where Norway is a creditor nation on a massive scale.[285] The net assets of the nation as a whole, known as the net investment position, shows that the country has amassed ownership of bonds, equities and real estate around the world worth 6239 billion krone ($734 billion) in net terms, a figure that has more than doubled between December 2010 and December 2014.[286] As a share of GDP, Norway's net international assets have also risen spectacularly, from around 100 per cent in 2011 to 185 per cent in 2016. Why such a sharp rise? A small part reflects the long-term investment strategy, but a much larger part shows the wisdom of investing its entire oil savings in foreign currency. In a period of sliding oil prices, Norway's flexible exchange rate falls in step, which means that its foreign currency assets suddenly become worth a great deal more when converted back into krone. Had Norway joined the euro it would not have had this flexibility. Instead, its membership of the Agreement on the European Economic Area (EEA) allows Norway to take part in the EU internal market. A less flexible exchange rate would also have meant higher inflation during the boom years. This long-term strategy, which converts non-renewable resources into a permanent financial asset, is so cleverly designed that even in the worst of times it becomes a veri- table cash cow that can be used to boost the economy. Norway is perhaps the only country in the world that can claim to have truly conquered the curse of plenty.

9

THE NEW NORTH

'I never believed that my government actually would do such a thing. We need to make them stop. The short-sightedness and the stupidity of it just makes me want to cry.'

Norwegian author Karl Ove Knausgård

IN THE HALF-CENTURY THAT NORWAY HAS LICENSED THE drilling of more than 5000 North Sea oil wells and produced 39 billion barrels of oil,[287] the planet has warmed considerably and the climate has become more unstable. Carbon dioxide concentration in the atmosphere has risen more than 20 per cent over this period, and extreme weather events are now the norm. In more recent decades, the science has confirmed fears that burning fossil fuel has dangerous consequences for humanity in the event that this warming triggers a tipping point, such as the release of vast amounts of methane from thawing permafrost. And even though Norway has been a torchbearer for international humanitarian efforts since the end of the Second World War, there's no question of its moving away from an oil-dependent economy. In fact, the country is on track to produce a great deal more oil and gas in the decades to come. It has now offered new licences in deeper and colder waters in the Arctic region. Evidently, the cohesive nature of society may be ruptured by the unresolved tensions between environmentalists and developers.

Norway's so-called 'red-green' agenda, which adds environmental measures to sweeten a pro-oil strategy, was there for all to see at the Paris climate summit in 2015 when the foreign minister Børge Brende hosted a side event to raise awareness about the dangers facing the Arctic region. He warned that temperatures in the region are rising two to three times faster than the global average and that this had implications for the Arctic and every part of the world:

> The ice in the Arctic cools our planet. If the ice caps melt, the sea level will rise by seven metres. And the Arctic permafrost traps huge amounts of CO_2 and methane, which will be released if it thaws. Rising temperatures in the Arctic will accelerate global warming and have an enormous impact on trade, migration, humanitarian crises, armed conflicts and global security. It is crucial that we act now.[288]

Elsewhere, Brende has explained how Norway sees the retreat of Arctic ice as both a threat to humanity and an opportunity for new economic frontiers, including oil and gas development. As he wrote in a 2015 article in the *Harvard International Review*: 'As the ice retreats, the Arctic countries will no longer be divided by the ice, but connected by the ocean. The sea will become a highway, not a barrier. It will open up new possibilities for trade and transport; mining and minerals; oil and gas; research and education.'[289]

This view is not just held by those on the Norwegian right. Even Norwegian greens think that burning more Norwegian oil is in the interest of humanity. One-time petroleum and energy minister and leading environmentalist Ane Hansdatter Kismul, who in her youth protested against controversial oil projects, says that Norway's oil is needed to prevent the planet warming beyond two degrees Celsius.[290] Without it, even more carbon-intensive fuel will be burned, she explains. Kismul was speaking in 2013 in her capacity as secretary of state for energy and petroleum in the former Labour government, a role she gained after cutting her political teeth on Norway's green movement. Perhaps she was simply stating the line of the 'red-green' government at the time. However, Kismul says she is opposed to oil exploration and development in sensitive areas such as the Lofoten and Vesterålen islands, together known as the LoVe islands, which have immense marine life and attract tourists in large numbers. But not so the oil companies, which have been pushing the Conservative and Progress parties to open up these areas.

The oil companies, including Statoil, want to drill around the LoVe islands and push further north into the Arctic. Politicians on both the left and right in Norway are willing to oblige by licensing new development in the Arctic region and by gaining control of new maritime territory. Fredrik Hagemann, Norway's first and most highly regarded petroleum geologist, who headed the NPD from its creation in 1972 until 1996, believes the Barents Sea has great petroleum potential and should be developed. 'I've always maintained that we can't write off the Barents Sea. We've only made some pinpricks there. Interest vanished for a while, but it's back again now,' he said.[291] Norway already has one of the biggest maritime zones in the world, but in 2006 the government led by Jens Stoltenberg applied to the UN Commission on the Limits of the Continental Shelf to extend Norway's Exclusive Economic Zone beyond its 200 nautical mile limit in the Northeast Atlantic and Arctic oceans and the Barents Sea. The commission approved the application in 2009, thereby adding another 235,000 square kilometres to Norway's maritime area. At the time, Norway's economic and fisheries zones amounted to a mammoth 4.3 million square kilometres, or more than ten times the land area. The commission's approval, followed by a 2010 boundary agreement with Russia, brings this total to 6.6 million square kilometres, or an area almost the size of the Australian continent.[292]

But there's growing discontent among many prominent Norwegians about the ethics of this push into a pristine environment, one that is already being harmed by rising levels of carbon dioxide in the atmosphere. In late 2015, a group of 200 leading Norwegian figures and organisations signed a petition calling on the government to halt its licensing of oil exploration and development in the Barents Sea, which followed just two years after the maritime boundary agreement with Russia was ratified by both parliaments. One of the signatories was Norway's towering literary great, the six-foot four-inch Karl Ove Knausgård, whose six-volume, 3600-page *My Struggle* has been translated into twenty-two languages. Knausgård's life bears some similarities to that of another Norwegian great, Edvard Munch, given that his work draws on his relationship with an abusive and alcoholic father while living on a remote island in southern Norway. After graduating from the University of Bergen, Knausgård held various jobs during his twenties, including pouring concrete on the giant Condeep platforms,[293] but now he says there is nothing noble about the country's drive to extract more oil in the Arctic region. For Knausgård and many others, it simply beggars belief that their country, which has prided itself on being a good international citizen for so long, would do such a thing:

> Norway is one of the richest countries in the world – it's all about greed, and it's a fucking disgrace. The Arctic is one of the few places left on the planet that still is unexploited, it's a very sensitive area, and I never believed that my government actually would do such a thing. We need to make them stop, and we still can do that … The short-sightedness and the stupidity of it just makes me want to cry.[294]

The petition says that Norway's 'business-as-usual extraction on the Norwegian Continental Shelf contradicts the precautionary principle and climate scientists' warnings'. 'Opening new areas of the Arctic for oil exploration would make Norway one of the frontrunners in a fossil-fuelled race towards an uninhabitable planet.' It is a precursor to taking legal action against the government, aimed at declaring that the drive north is unconstitutional. Article 112 of Norway's constitution states that, as with the financial management of oil revenue, the government needs to take into account the impact of natural resource use on future generations. The article states:

> Natural resources shall be managed on the basis of comprehensive long-term considerations which will safeguard this right for future generations as well. In order to safeguard their right in accordance with the foregoing paragraph, citizens are entitled to information on the state of the natural environment and on the effects of any encroachment on nature that is planned or carried out.

The local backlash has coincided with the attack on coal companies by the Norwegian parliament and government. While it's true that coal is more carbon intensive than oil, the timing of these actions seems ironic given that Norway is copping political heat at home about its march into the Arctic region. As NBIM said in explaining the decision, the reasons for divesting from coal companies include 'long-established climate-change risk-management expectations', even though the same could be said for further oil development, especially in the Arctic region.

The petition followed the Conservative government's decision in January 2015 to offer new rights in the Barents Sea in what was the first offering of frontier acreage in twenty-one years. Norway first approved development of the south-western part of this remote region as early as 1979. This led to two developments at the very top of Norway's northern coastline. The first, Snøhvit, which was discovered in 1984, proved to be a major find at around one-third the size of Ekofisk. When it went into production in 2007 it became the northern-most oilfield in the world, relying on the longest multiphase pipeline for transporting unprocessed gas, water and hydrocarbons. The second field, the much smaller Goliat, was discovered in 2000 and is due to commence production in 2016. These finds have raised high hopes among oil companies of even bigger discoveries, notwithstanding the high cost of development. The conclusion of forty years of negotiations with Russia over the maritime boundary in 2010 allowed the Conservative government to renew the push northwards by including exploration blocks in the Barents Sea in its latest licensing round, the twenty-third launched so far.

The Barents Sea is a sub-Arctic sea that in the east extends along the top half of Norway, all the way north to seventy-four degrees latitude, just below the Arctic ice. In the west, the Barents laps the northern coast of Greenland. While this area is part of the Arctic region, the warm water from the Gulf Stream keeps the coast free of ice all year round, making it more accessible for development than the North American and Russian Arctic regions.[295] Thirty years of exploration in the western part of the Barents has led to thirty-nine discoveries.[296]

This new frontier poses considerable risks for oil companies, however. As Norway's Petroleum Safety Authority put it in a review of the exploration effort: 'Everyone wants to head for the far north. The question is whether all of them are ready to go.'[297] As the petroleum minister Tord Lien admits, the region is 'high cost, high risk'.[298] The 24-hour darkness during the winter months makes the Barents a formidable working environment, thus underscoring yet again the extremes that humanity is willing to take to extract oil. But the challenges are not insurmountable. Lien explains: 'There has been oil and gas activity in the Arctic for almost 100 years.

Norwegian Arctic waters are totally different from Alaska and Canada. The temperature is not comparable. I was born in the Arctic. Five hundred thousand people live in the Arctic region. You have the challenge with the light, the darkness in winter makes some of the work more challenging. I'm not trying to underestimate that you have risks but it's nothing we can't handle.'

Despite the sliding oil price, companies are responding enthusiastically to the government's development agenda. A record number of exploration wells are now set to be drilled in the area as a result of the new licences. Given the environmental and safety risks posed by these developments, it has to be asked whether Norway's regulatory regime needs to be strengthened and made more independent. Norway's supposedly independent oil administration, now divided into the Petroleum Safety Authority (PSA) and the NPD, no longer operates under an independent board, conceivably exposing it to government pressure to approve risky fields. But as Lien explains, the decisions the directorates make are made public, obviating the need for independent boards: 'As with all directorates, they take their decisions. What they communicate to me is public. The system in place works really well. Most of the time they make the decision,' he says. However, there are concerns that the government's drive to encourage more medium-size companies onto the Norwegian Continental Shelf to compete against the oil majors, and Statoil, results in less stringent environmental assessments. This appears to be the case with a new award system known as 'awards in pre-defined areas' (APA), which involves offering blocks to smaller companies in mature areas. In these awards, environmental evaluations are reportedly less stringent. There have been numerous instances whereby the NPD has failed to take into account concerns raised by Norway's Institute of Marine Research.[299] A committee appointed in 2010 to review this system concluded that the introduction of APAs had been a mistake, but even so the government continues to make these awards.

Anne Myhrvold, director general of the PSA, agrees that the push into the Barents will stretch existing boundaries of technology and competence, and says that industry will have to work together to find solutions. Myhrvold, who came to the role with twenty years of experience in the private sector, including at BP and in research institutes, says: 'The operational conditions in the Barents Sea are different and may call for different solutions in order to ensure regulatory compliance. Industry standards play an important role here. There is consensus between the authorities and the industry that there is a need for further development and improvement of relevant standards. The main challenges are long distances and lack of infrastructure, combined with harsh weather conditions and total darkness during a part of the year.'[300]

Myhrvold is now one of two women working at the very top of Norway's oil administration. While things were run in the early days by Norway's few good men, women are now moving into the top positions, with one exception being NBIM, which has no women on its senior management team. The NPD's director general is Bente Nyland, a geologist, who has run the organisation since 2008, and three of the four members in the senior management team are also women. Myhrvold says that despite the improvement in safety over the past decade, she cannot rule out a disaster on the scale of BP's *Deepwater Horizon*: 'Despite all efforts to operate safely, there is always a risk involved. We can therefore not claim that a major accident cannot happen. The PSA carefully assessed all recommendations that emerged from the *Deepwater Horizon* investigations. We found that the majority of the recommendations were already accounted for in our regulatory approach, but we did implement some recommendations that we found relevant and useful.'

Finn Carlsen, the PSA's director of professional competence, who has had a long career as a safety regulator, says that the plan to open up the Barents involved a thorough assessment within the government. He points out that aside from the issue of darkness, the Barents is not dissimilar from many other parts of the Norwegian Continental Shelf where companies have been operating for decades: 'The northern limit of areas that are opened in Barents Sea is at 74°30'. Despite the high altitude, there is no permanent sea ice in the area, icebergs are rarely observed, and sea temperature is not lower than further south. All this is mainly because of the Gulf Stream. However, low air temperatures combined with strong wind can cause heavy icing on installations and vessels. The cold as well as the winter darkness is also a challenge for workers. Another typical and challenging weather phenomenon in the Barents Sea is rapid weather changes, often difficult to predict.'[301]

The Arctic has been heralded as the next big frontier for oil exploration, with the region estimated to hold some 13 per cent of the world's undiscovered oil and 30 per cent of its undiscovered gas. Jez Averty, Statoil's vice president for exploration in Norway, said the acreage in the twenty-third licensing round offered 'significant volume potential, but never-the-less there is a debate where some say that these resources will not be commercial'. He said that new technology would help to reduce the cost of producing the 'significant discoveries we hope to make in the Barents Sea'.[302] In addition to exploiting the Barents, Statoil argues there is a strong case for further exploration in the LoVe islands area. 'Statoil thinks it's important to start exploring this area to determine future resources potential,' a company spokesperson says.[303]

As with earlier developments on the Norwegian Continental Shelf, cooperation is the key to reducing production costs. Statoil is one of sixteen companies to have formed the Barents Sea Exploration Collaboration project, which is aimed at finding common solutions to reduce costs and establish good safety practices. Statoil was the lead company in a group of thirty-three that cooperated on seismic surveys in the licensing area.

The Norwegian government seems pretty pleased with the response from business so far to this new round. Following the 2 December 2015 deadline for exploration bids, the NPD said that twenty-six companies had applied for acreage, ranging from the big majors such as Chevron, Shell and ConocoPhillips, to the emerging businesses such as Sweden's Lundin Petroleum. The licensing round comprised fifty-seven announced blocks or parts of blocks, with three in the Norwegian Sea and fifty-four in the Barents Sea. Of these fifty-four blocks, thirty-four are located in the newly opened area in the south-eastern Barents Sea, and many of the applications target this acreage. This is indeed a significant level of interest at a time of low oil prices, indicating that most businesses believe the recent price slump will be short-lived. Additional awards in 2015 through the APA process resulted in eleven exploration blocks awarded in the Barents Sea, and thirty-five in the Norwegian Sea immediately to the south. The round resulted in the government awarding ten new licences in May 2016, all of them in the Barents Sea, including three in the newly opened area in the southeast. Statoil was awarded the role of operator, or lead contractor, in four of these blocks, and Lundin was made operator in a further three. Another three smaller oil companies were made operators. The Big Oil companies that are partners in these consortiums include Chevron, ConocoPhillips and Japan's Idemitsu.[304]

Wood Mackenzie, an energy consulting firm, has argued that the costs of exploration are considerably lower in the Norwegian Barents compared with other sub-Arctic regions, and this explains why there has been so much interest. Andrew Latham, vice president of exploration, said that after taking generous tax concessions into account, the cost per exploration well in the Norwegian Barents might be as low as $20 million, twenty times lower than drilling in the Russian and Alaskan offshore Arctic during 2014–15, and five to ten times lower than drilling in offshore Greenland during 2010–11.[305] These figures attest to the fact that despite the high nominal tax rate, the Norwegian government offers generous incentives to encourage more oil development.

Statoil is pushing into other extreme areas around the world, both in the far north and the far south of the planet. In the wild waters of Australia's Southern Ocean, which are buffeted by the Roaring Forties, Statoil has joined with BP to invest around $1 billion in an exploration program. So far, Australia's offshore regulator NOPSEMA has rejected the application to drill on environmental grounds. Pål Haremo, Statoil's vice president for exploration in Australasia, says the area known as the Ceduna Basin is one of the world's last remaining unexplored frontiers. The water depths in the region being targeted by the consortium reach more than 2000 metres, making it a very high-cost operation. Haremo explains: 'The risk is so high. We need a portfolio of licences for success in one area. Ceduna is one of around twenty basins in the world that are considered frontier. We don't expect all of them to be successful. In five years there might only be four to five [offshore basins] left to drill outside the Arctic and Antarctic. Australia is big and still has potential.'[306]

So far, this high-risk approach has paid off, as Statoil has emerged in recent years as one of the most successful explorers in the world, with a reserve replacement rate around 120 per cent in the three years to the end of 2014. Statoil has for decades been able to push the technical limits of oil discovery, but this national champion is now testing the threshold of political tolerance.

SUCCESS AND DEPENDENCY

When the International Monetary Fund reviewed the Norwegian economy in 2015, it found a country that was in a vastly better economic position than any other European nation, and indeed any other oil-rich country. But it was not a country without problems. Norway had not completely escaped the ill-effects of the decade-long oil boom, as shown by the inflated cost of housing, labour, and goods and services. Norway has the second-highest per capita GDP in the world, $97,000, according to the latest World Bank data. Asked if Norway had avoided Dutch disease, the central bank governor Øystein Olsen concedes that its savings strategy has meant that it has avoided it in a financial sense, but not entirely in an economic sense, given the oil sector had caused the non-oil economy to contract, which is known as crowding out. Olsen explains: 'Depending on how you define Dutch disease. The answer is yes if you look at spending oil revenues to the extent that we have done. [But] we have very profitable activities in the oil sector. The oil sector is paying high wages – that has the crowding-out effect. We have avoided Dutch disease in the sense we have not gone too far. It is necessary to have some crowding out. Since the 1990s we have had full employment and continuous growth, and high productivity growth in the mainland economy. So the last twenty years have been quite successful, and we have benefited from our petroleum resources.'[307]

The same can't be said for other resource-rich countries that have spent all of the windfall revenue from their commodity booms. A graph used by Olsen in a 2014 speech showed that while Norway's terms of trade had increased more than Australia's since 1999, Norway's real exchange rate had remained relatively stable, while Australia's had increased by about 40 per cent.[308] That is, while both countries have experienced sharply rising prices for their commodity exports, Norway's wealth fund had the effect of depressing the exchange rate to some degree, given that the country invests all the assets in foreign currency. Olsen explains: 'Compared with other commodity-based economies, like Canada, Australia and New Zealand, fluctuations in the real exchange rate have been moderate. The build-up of the fund may have helped contain a temporary real appreciation during a period of high oil revenues.'

As a result of this savings policy, Norway's pension fund is predicted to peak at around 160–170 per cent of GDP in coming decades, and after that it will gradually decline as a share of GDP as the economy grows. Olsen argues that while the country has accumulated a 'big fortune', it will in the future have to base its prosperity on human capital and technology.

But another channel for Dutch disease to take hold is through the financial sector, which in Norway has led to soaring house prices and increased leverage and risk for borrowers and lenders. As the IMF review explained, credit to the private sector grew by 6–7 per cent a year in the five years to 2014, with most of this money funnelled into a booming property market, especially in the oil towns along the west coast. This means that despite the immense benefit derived from the wealth fund and the absence of public-sector debt, Norway has indeed experienced its own economic bubble and this now poses a serious risk to the economy, just as it did in the early 1990s. The IMF said 'continued vigilance and proactive efforts toward mitigating systemic risks are warranted', and it called for the financial regulator, the FSA, to carry out 'stress tests' on banks and to monitor interbank lending. Norway introduced financial sector reforms in July 2015 for mortgage lenders, but the IMF stated there was clearly a need for the entire regulatory regime to be strengthened, especially in the area of wholesale lending. The IMF also noted that the FSA should be given greater independence from government.

The government is well aware of the risks facing the economy from the exponential growth in house prices since the mid-2000s. Norges Bank deputy governor Jon Nicolaisen said following the release of the 2015 *Financial Stability Report* that while banks had increased their capital buffers, 'some aspects of the Norwegian economy are a source of vulnerability for banks'.[309]

Norway's success in building a manufacturing and services industry around its petroleum resources also means that it is more exposed in the event of a prolonged period of lower oil prices. As the IMF noted, the benefit the economy had generated from oil and gas investment made the country more vulnerable and this meant that Norway had to manage its 'oil dependency':

> Steadily increasing oil and gas investment over the last decade has provided persistent demand stimulus to the increasingly oil- and gas-focused mainland economy. However, investment flattened out last year and is expected to decline significantly in the coming years, and impulse from the offshore sector to the mainland economy has turned from positive to negative. Oil and gas production will continue for many decades to come, so the problems of managing the oil dependency of the mainland economy are not yet over.[310]

As oil prices plummeted in early 2016, the exposure of highly leveraged borrowers in Oslo and in west coast oil towns became acute, in turn putting the entire financial system under considerable stress.

GLASS HALF FULL

It's hard to criticise Norway's approach to energy from a domestic consumption viewpoint, given that it produces a vast amount of hydro power that supplies electricity at home and is also exported to Europe. In 1991, Norway became one of the first countries in the world to put a price on carbon. In addition, its petroleum products are highly taxed. A litre of gas in Norway costs more than $2, making it one of the highest pump prices in the world. But the country's dependence on oil, and its approach to renewable energy, has led to criticism at home. Norwegian historian Helge Ryggvik observes that

Norway's dependence on oil is reflected in its lack of interest in developing new sources of renewable energy, most notably offshore wind. He wrote in a 2010 paper that while Denmark, Britain and Germany 'have developed a significant sustainable offshore windfarm industry, there is no comparable investment in Norway – despite the fact that the natural conditions are better in Norway'.[311] Even though the government has been making some effort on renewables, Ryggvik stood by this view in 2016.[312] He is highly critical of the former 'red-green' Labour government for going 'full speed ahead' with oil development while making a token effort on renewables. While the government increased clean energy–related research, this did not result in any significant investment in Norway, he notes. An agreement between Norway and Sweden to develop wind energy led to just one new project in Norway, with most of the investment going into Sweden even though Norway's vast coastline makes it better suited to wind power. The end result is that Sweden has around 10,000 gigawatt hours of wind power capacity, more than five times that of Norway. Denmark has also made great strides, with more than 11,000 gigawatt hours of wind power capacity. International Energy Agency data shows that while 96 per cent of Norway's electricity is produced by hydro power, just 1.4 per cent is generated by wind power.[313]

The petroleum and energy minister Tord Lien finds a question about this issue somewhat offensive. He contends that Norway is one of only two countries in the world that sources almost 100 per cent of its domestic power from renewable sources, and it is also exporting its renewable technology around the world: 'We are increasing the export capacity to Germany and the UK. We are licensing wind power everywhere at a speed that has never happened. We have delivered licences for more than eleven terawatt hours. I already ask Norwegian taxpayers for an extra tax for renewables, I can't ask them to pay more because the Europeans are subsidising their energy system.'[314]

While it's true that Norway's hydro power exceeds the renewable energy generated in neighbouring countries, the criticism still stands that Norway could have done much more to boost new sources of clean energy production had it not been so fixated on oil. Even though oil production peaked back in 2000 and has nearly halved since then, Norway's oil odyssey is far from over as the country continues to find new resources, especially gas.[315] Offsetting the slump in oil is a doubling of natural gas output over the same period so that overall sales of hydrocarbons have held up. Norway's gas production is ranked seventh-largest in the world, although oil has slipped to sixteenth.[316] Gas production overtook that of oil in 2011, and even though overall hydrocarbon production peaked in 2004,[317] the latest figures show it is running at just 20 per cent below that peak level.[318] Projections for the rest of this decade show that petroleum production is expected to increase slightly, with oil production holding steady while gas increases. The International Energy Agency forecasts only a 'slight decline' in the Norwegian gas supply between now and 2040.[319]

The Norwegian government estimates that its discovered petroleum resources on the continental shelf amount to around 71 billion barrels of oil. Of this, 55 per cent has already been sold and delivered. The Norwegian Petroleum Museum has estimates that if the produced barrels were stacked on top of each other, they could reach the moon fifteen times. But there are another 31 billion barrels of known reserves, while the official estimates add a further 18 billion barrels of 'undiscovered' resources, giving a total resource of 88 billion barrels. Based on the current rate of extraction, this would mean Norway still has another twenty-three years of oil and gas production, but new discoveries have been offsetting around half of this production level, which is clearly what the drive into the Barents is all about. If this rate of discovery is maintained, the time horizon could be extended for another fifty years.[320] The NPD says there is no international standard for adding estimates of undiscovered reserves to the country's energy inventory. An NPD spokesperson indicated that Norway was simply following the practice of many countries around the world, and of companies that report to stock exchanges. 'Many countries make evaluations of their undiscovered resources, but it may not be published together with the discovered resources as we do regularly in Norway. There is no international standard on this reporting practice for nations as [there] is for companies who report to stock exchanges.'[321] Global estimates produced by BP indicate a less optimistic scenario when applying a narrower definition of proved reserves. The *BP Statistical Review of World Energy*, which has been published for the past sixty-four years, ranks Norway's proved reserves at just 7 billion barrels of oil.[322] When compared to the rate of production, these reserves indicate a life expectancy of just nine and a half years.

Norway hasn't discovered a super-giant field since the late 1970s, the last one being Troll, but in 2010 the Swedish company Lundin Petroleum found the medium-size Johan Sverdrup field in a well-explored area 155 kilometres directly east of Stavanger. This field extends over 200 square kilometres in an area that has been extensively explored since the 1960s, so the find shows that new technology can turn up significant resources. Johan Sverdrup is exactly half the size of Ekofisk, though it seems the days of turning up super-giant fields are probably over.

Even though Norway can be criticised for having extracted its petroleum too quickly, especially after creating the sovereign wealth fund, the country has certainly done better than the United Kingdom. The UK's remaining oil reserves are less than half the size of Norway's, even though the two countries have produced almost identical amounts of oil. Since the beginning of North Sea oil production to the end of 2014, Norway's oil production has averaged 76,272 barrels per day, compared with 77,156 for the UK.[323] The UK has produced more natural gas than Norway in the years from 1970 to 2014: 2.446 billion cubic metres to Norway's 1.850 billion cubic metres. Today, Norway's proven gas reserves stand at 2 trillion cubic metres, or ten times the reserves of the UK. Norway's reserves to production rate stands at 17.7 years, compared with 6.6 for the UK. This starkly different bottom line in part reflects the divergent strategies taken by the two countries in the early years, with the UK opting for a much faster rate of extraction. So while Norway could have earned better financial returns had it left more of its resources in the ground, the results of its natural resource stewardship are stark when compared with the UK and other resource-rich countries. Not only has it left more of its resources in the ground, it has created a financial endowment that will continue to earn income for the country long after the last oil and gas well has run dry, or if the country decides to draw the line and leave resources unextracted. Projections published by the central bank indicate that Norway's GPFG is on track to surpass the trillion-dollar mark by 1 January 2019, based on the May 2016 dollar-krone exchange rate. While this estimate is no doubt subject to fluctuations in the oil price and the US dollar, it remains a significant achievement that far surpasses the performance of other resource-rich nations.

Despite the international prestige that Norway continues to accumulate from its stored wealth, technological mastery and humanitarian record, the drive into the new north risks creating a significant blemish on its reputation as an exemplary nation. What's worse is that while Norway has condemned other producers of fossil fuel, it now seriously risks being seen as a nation that is willing to exploit the adverse side-effects of human-induced climate change.

10

NORDIC RULES FOR RICHES

IN SCANDINAVIAN COUNTRIES GENERALLY, THE HARSH climate means that people tend to pull together and support each other, so this might explain in part why Norway has done much better than many other resource-rich countries, including other developed nations, in achieving a consensus on the fundamental basis for developing its petroleum wealth. While it's true that other resource-rich countries are more diverse and more politically divided, there's still a great deal of common sense and good practice that can be learned from Norway's fifty years of intense debate, policy formulation and much trial and error.

OWN THE RESOURCE

One factor that sets Norway apart is the universally accepted idea of state ownership. This was the view that Norwegians took in the early 1900s when they negotiated concessions for development of their hydro resources, and it's very much the view they took from the 1960s onwards, even though Norway's need for foreign capital put it in a weak starting position. Norwegians quickly developed the view that the government should control the resource's development in order to ensure that extraction led to the betterment of Norwegian society. This contrasts with the debate in other resource-rich countries where companies are seen as benefactors who are doing the country a favour by developing resources, often with substantial tax concessions. The narrative in these countries, even those with democratic institutions, is limited to the notion that these developments will generate jobs for the country's population. The most advantageous starting point for the licensing and management of any mineral or energy concession is the notion that the resources belong to the state and that it's the government that can decide how best to develop them.

PLAN FOR THE UNEXPECTED

When Norway first began designing its sovereign wealth fund, no-one thought that it would amount to very much, given the parlous state of government finances at the time and the outlook for oil prices. But in the space of a few years things turned around and the fund began soaring in value, thus demonstrating the dividends gained from putting in place sound arrangements. Periods of depressed commodity prices, as currently prevail, can be the ideal time to begin planning for when things might turn around. And it's at these times that reforms to taxation arrangements, especially the imposition of additional taxes on profits, can be more easily digested by industry. When these additional taxes kicked in, the returns to the Norwegian state were handsome indeed, especially given the fact that country had dispensed with its production-based royalties in order to raise revenue solely through profits-based taxes.

COOPERATION IS KING

The Norwegian business empires developed on the back of the oil wealth from the 1970s onwards proved that a small country could leverage its primary commodity in order to develop onshore industry. But for a relatively small country to succeed, industry needed to work together, and this cooperative approach has been the driver of success over the past twenty years. Jens Stoltenberg, who served as petroleum minister in the early 1990s, realised that Norway had developed considerable expertise in the oil and gas industries, in part with protectionist policies, and that it had to move beyond the local market in order to survive and prosper. Instead of going it alone, Stoltenberg pushed government and industry to work together to take their technology to the world.

The result of this cooperative approach is more than 3000 oil service businesses, which now employ around 300,000 people, or one in nine Norwegian jobs.[324] Over the past decade this industry has been earning more export income than gas exports. While many of these businesses are now under pressure as a result of the collapsing oil price, it's clear that Norway has developed cutting-edge technology and expertise in the offshore industry. As *The Economist's* correspondent wrote in 1975, this industry will be generating income for the country long after the oil and gas has been depleted.

Pål Helsing, the president of Kongsberg Oil and Gas Technologies, says, 'The North Sea was very special. It had deep water, harsh environment; new technology had to be developed in Norway using the skill base and the universities and the research institutes and the industry in collaboration.' Speaking during a Norwegian royal visit to Australia in 2015, Helsing explained: 'The oil and gas industry had reached a certain level; it was seen that we had to take what had been developed in the North Sea and get that sold to the larger market. It was an initiative of the authorities, the government and industry, Statoil and the industrial companies, to use the joint force, a Team Norway type of approach, and move this into the world. And today as an industrial group our [export] revenue is exceeding the domestic revenue. As you have seen today we manage to engage the government, and even the royal family is engaged to attract and be a kind of spearhead for the Norwegian industry as a whole. I think it is a fantastic thing to do.'[325]

This ethos can be found in the practices of some of the country's wealthiest entrepreneurs. Kjell Inge Røkke, who overcame dyslexia to make his fortune with a fleet of fishing boats, bought the Aker shipping company, which he renamed Aker Solutions. When Aker's 50 per cent–owned subsidiary Det Norske chose an Asian shipyard to build the platforms for the Ivar Aasen field, Røkke sacked its board.[326] Norwegian content in the more recent fields remains very high. For ENI's development of the Goliat field in the Barents Sea, the heavy engineering work was done in South Korea while the technology was developed in Norway, lifting overall Norwegian content to 65 per cent.

Norway's team approach reflects more than cultural factors. As the petroleum minister Tord Lien notes, tax incentives and government directives also drove cooperation: 'One of the key success factors in Norway has been, from the very beginning, that we nurture our companies to work together. When we have created licences there are always two, three or four companies. We have created a fiscal framework that stimulates cooperation. The fiscal system stimulates research and development. We have fiscal support for high-risk research and early development.'[327]

SKILLS ARE ENABLERS

Norway's industrial success has been underpinned by the ready availability of a well-trained workforce, which was able to hit the ground running and supply skilled labour and expertise to this emerging industry. This reflected the skills base that the country had accumulated as a result of its shipping and hydro-electric industries, but even this amount of human capital might not have been sufficient had it not been for the country's emphasis on having its people trained in universities and in workplaces, at home and abroad. Around the world, universities can be slow to swing with the changing times, but in Norway the universities switched very quickly. Arve Johnsen's insistence on sending new recruits to work in foreign oil companies also proved to be a decisive way of upskilling Norwegians, as well as teaching them a great deal about how this complex and often opaque industry really worked.

Norway's skills base means it remains competitive in producing high-quality hardware for the shipping and petroleum industries, despite having the highest labour cost in the world. This explains why Rolls-Royce Marine, which services the shipping and petroleum industries, has around 2700 employees in Norway. The family-owned shipbuilding company Kleven is one business that has in recent years reversed its earlier decisions to send production offshore. Trond Liavaag, managing director of Kleven Maritime Technology, says the firm combines good technology, well-trained staff and effective processes to remain globally competitive while based in Norway. 'The key word is to be effective. With very good planning we can do it best in Norway. We have good tools, a good routine and good equipment,' he says. [328] The company has previously had sections of its ships made in Poland, but now it is now bringing more production back to its two yards in Norway: 'We are trying to take home much more of the production. Then we will have full control and it is much more effective. The most important thing is to deliver the job exactly on schedule. If you order in China you can't be certain of that,' says Liavaag. He says the role of government in the early days of the oil industry was important for helping manufacturers to win contracts, though now Norwegian companies are internationally competitive and need no such support. Kleven's order list, which is published on its website, shows the planned delivery of eighteen ships in 2016 and 2017, all of them built in shipyards in Norway.

SAFETY IN TEAMS

Norway learned the hard way about the cost of rushing development and allowing companies to take an authoritarian approach in risky working conditions. The lives lost in workplace accidents in the first two decades of oil development also reflected the failure of the government authorities to effectively regulate the industry. Safety is not determined by the number of inspections carried out in any given period; it reflects the extent to which workers, employers and regulators are able to communicate openly and effectively about the risks they face. This approach appears to have led to a sustained reduction in workplace accidents and deaths in the North Sea, and in the Norwegian sector especially. Although, as the Petroleum Safety Authority's director general Anne Myhrvold concedes, no-one can say never in relation to safety, and this is especially the case as the country moves its search for oil into colder and darker regions in the new Arctic. In 2010, Norway experienced a near miss in its Gullfaks operation, when a kink in the well could have turned into a major accident. While a serious accident can't be ruled out, there's no doubt that the team approach is helping to allow this hazardous industry to operate in a more acceptable way. Accidents on the scale of the *Kielland* and *Piper Alpha* have been avoided, but the necessity of air travel to and from platforms continues to make the North Sea a dangerous place to operate. The UK's incomplete data indicates that more than 110 lives have been lost in air crashes relating to oil and gas operations over the past four decades (see Appendix B). Norway's air toll is considerably lower, but there can never be cause for complacency. A seven-year stretch without a major incident ended in April 2016 when a helicopter returning from the Gullfaks operation crashed near Bergen, killing all thirteen on board.

INVEST WISELY AND ETHICALLY

Norway isn't the only country in the world with significant financial capital, but it's certainly one country that is showing how it can get more bang from its bucks. There is much more to life than accumulating financial assets, and as pension funds grow around the world, more of these investors could learn how non-monetary returns from the way this capital is used can indeed be very rewarding. Norway could have simply been a lazy index investor, but one intangible reason for taking the direct investment approach has been the extra-monetary benefit of being able to exercise direct control over the investments, and to help make the world a better place. Not only has Norway been able to accumulate massive wealth with its astute policies, it has also been able to project influence well beyond its population size by taking an active and ethical approach to investment.

HEDGE AGAINST THE DOWNSIDE

Perhaps the most powerful lesson of all to emerge from Norway's experience is its practice of investing all of its oil-related savings in foreign currency. This strict rule has meant the country has spent at a sustainable rate and saved in a way that will protect the country's economy during a downturn. When the price of oil crashes, the currencies of oil producers also fall in step. This means the value of Norway's savings when converted back to krone increases with the falling exchange rate. This gives Norway additional financial firepower to ward off a widespread economic downturn. While it can be said that Norway has relied too heavily on the oil industry, this financial strength will allow the country to weather downturns and diversify its economy – hopefully to one that is less carbon intensive.

AFTERWORD

Had a little smart thinking been applied, Australia's biggest and longest ride on the resources rollercoaster since the 1850s gold rush could have been very beneficial indeed. If federal and state governments had put a share of their windfall revenue into a foreign currency future fund, thereby taking advantage of record-high mineral prices and the soaring Australian dollar, they would have amassed a tidy fortune. Today, when converted back into local currency, this stockpile of wealth would be worth much more than the capital outlaid, given that the Australian dollar has naturally fallen in step with sliding mineral prices. These savings could have been used to boost the economy after the mineral boom, obviating the need for governments, and the nation, to go further into debt.

Instead, hundreds of billions of dollars in windfall government revenue have been spectacularly squandered. Now, at the end of this feast-to-famine feeding frenzy, there's no prospect of the federal government paying down its $A325 billion net debt, which is likely to continue rising for the rest of the decade. Australia owes the world more than $A1 trillion in net terms, two and a half times the amount owed at the start of the boom.

Australia's lack of planning and foresight during this episode appears to reflect our British heritage. As shown in these pages, Britain disastrously mismanaged its North Sea oil bounty from the 1970s onwards, in sharp contrast to the measured, controlled and long-term strategy adopted at the same time on the other side of the North Sea in Norway. Australia's policy settings similarly fail to register three fundamental truths about the resources industry: that companies profit from extracting the minerals belonging to the Australian people; that these resources are finite; and that price booms never last.

Australian governments, especially during boom times, have consistently operated as though none of these factors apply. This approach has been reinforced by economic advisers and media commentators. Treasury documents released to me under the freedom of information law reveal that the treasurer was advised by his department in June 2007 that the rise in national income from the mining boom, then in its fourth year, could be considered 'permanent'. Treasury then said this provided a 'strong case for spending additional revenue'. Influential economic commentators even chastised the treasury for having failed to predict the mining boom, therefore denying Australians an even bigger round of tax cuts. According to a treasury research paper, the Howard government spent more than 90 per cent of a $334 billion revenue windfall in its last three years in office – on tax cuts and middle-class welfare.

Labor's planning was flawed too. In 2008 Prime Minister Kevin Rudd held his 2020 Summit. The summit was supposed to raise issues affecting our future prosperity, yet policies to better manage the mining boom weren't mentioned in the economic discussion led by the treasurer, or in the 400-page report that followed. The lack of strategic thinking is astonishing, especially when compared with the considered analysis and long-term planning that prevailed at the start of Norway's oil boom. The Labor government did try to introduce a super-profits tax in 2010, which treasury sources said could have raised $100 billion over a decade. This income was not earmarked for a sovereign wealth fund, but would at least have delivered more of the profit to the nation, rather than to the mostly foreign-owned mining corporations. However, the design of the tax was overly complex and its hasty introduction allowed the mining companies to ambush the government. In what must be one of the most comprehensive policy defeats since Federation, the miners knocked off the prime minister and then killed the tax, thanks in part to an advertising blitz costing a mere $22 million. Research commissioned by Big Dirt showed that the ads' rhetoric convinced the Australian people that the nation's prosperity was dependent on its lightly taxed mining sector. (Stock-exchange data indicates that the effective tax rate on the resources sector is around 30 per cent, less than half Norway's rate, and lower even than that of some emerging economies.)

There are two key lessons for Australia from the story of Norwegian oil. First, the government should revisit the super-profits tax, so that the nation benefits the next time mineral prices surge. In order to head off the political opportunists, the government must properly explain the need for this tax, and perhaps package it with reform of imposts such as stamp duty and royalties that are legacies of our colonial past. Even though China's demand for coal and iron ore may have peaked, India is likely to sustain demand for these key commodities for many years to come. A period of low commodity prices provides an opportunity to introduce such a reform, notwithstanding the likely backlash from a diminished mining industry. Second, this revenue should be channelled into a foreign currency fund to hedge against the next commodity downturn.

The really big lesson from Norway is not the size of its trillion dollar fund; it is the way every single krone of surplus revenue has been converted into foreign currency. Norway has a commodity-based economy like Australia's, but it has built a giant hedge to help manage the boom times and protect against the inevitable periods of subdued commodity prices. This explains why Norway is a creditor nation that has almost doubled its net foreign assets to around

185 per cent of GDP since 2010. That is the equivalent of Australia having amassed net foreign assets worth $3 trillion; instead, we owe the world $1 trillion.

Neither the Australian government nor its private sector seems to understand the long-term benefit of building up a hedge against mineral downturns. Our much-vaunted $1.3 trillion in superannuation savings is massively over-invested in domestic assets, with only 30 per cent invested offshore. This industry, which has a guaranteed revenue stream as a result of government policy, failed to take advantage of the high Australian dollar as it surged above its long-term average of US70c and indeed went above $US1 at the height of the boom. Had these investment managers lifted their foreign currency allocation in step with the rising Australian dollar, the superannuation savings of all Australians would potentially be worth hundreds of billions of dollars more than they are today, and the financial pressure on retirees and government would be commensurately lower.

For most of our history, Australia has been dependent on the prices obtained from shipments of bulk commodities to earn export income. It is about time that we recognised this reality by putting in place a framework to ensure future generations will benefit from the extraction of our finite mineral resources.

APPENDIX A: NORWAY'S TEN OIL 'COMMANDMENTS'

Ten principles outlined in the *Storting (Parliament) White Paper*, Standing Committee of Industry, 14 June 1971:

1. Ensure national governance and control of the entire activity on the Norwegian Continental Shelf.

2. Exploit the petroleum deposits in such a manner that Norway minimizes its dependency on crude oil imports.

3. Develop new business activities based on the petroleum sector.

4. The development of the oil and gas industry must give necessary consideration to existing business and to the environment.

5. Flaring of valuable natural gas is not accepted on the Norwegian Continental Shelf, except for shorter test periods.

6. Petroleum from the Norwegian Continental Shelf shall as a main rule be shipped to Norway unless societal impact considerations require other alternatives.

7. The government shall be involved at all appropriate levels, contribute to the coordination of Norwegian interests within the Norwegian oil industry, and develop an integrated Norwegian petroleum environment with both national and international goals.

8. A state-owned oil company shall be established to secure the Government's economic interests, and to have a positive cooperation with national and foreign interests.

9. The activity north of 62 degrees shall satisfy the special societal impact conditions tied to this part of the country.

10. Future Norwegian petroleum discoveries may expose the Norwegian foreign policy to new challenges.

Translated in the report to the Storting (white paper) 2010–2011, An Industry for the Future – Norway's Petroleum Activities, Storting (Parliament of Norway), *p. 8.*

APPENDIX B: THE HUMAN COST OF NORTH SEA OIL

NORWAY

CAUSE	1967–79	1980s	1990s	2000s	2010–16
Structural failures	6	134	0	1	0
Helicopters	34	0	15	0	14
Falls	25	12	6	1	1
Diving	10	6	0	0	0
Lifting	3	0	2	3	0
Accidents on vessels	1	1	3	3	0
Fires and explosions	5	–	0	–	0
Drilling operations	0	1	3	0	0
Toxicity	3	1	0	0	0
Others	1	1	3	1	0
TOTAL	92	156	30	9	15

Source: Torgeir Moan, 2010, NTNU. Updated by author.

UNITED KINGDOM (INCOMPLETE SUMMARY)

CAUSE	1980s	1990s	2000s	2010–11 to 2013–14
'Offshore' accidents	167*	20	15	3
Helicopter	59	17	17	0
INCOMPLETE TOTAL	226	37	32	3

Sources: Offshore accidents, UK Health and Safety Executive from 1991 onwards. Helicopter accidents from: HSE, UK Offshore Public Transport Helicopter Safety Record (1976–2002), HSE, Norwich, 2004.

*1980s estimate comprised of *Piper Alpha* incident only.

APPENDIX C: THE NORTH SEA'S CONCRETE GIANTS

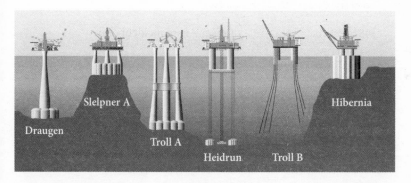

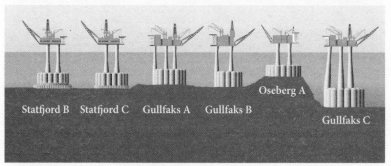

Cross section of some of the biggest and deepest concrete platforms installed on the Norwegian Continental Shelf. Troll was installed in 300 metres of water, and Heidrun in 350 metres. Source: Kværner AS.

APPENDIX D: COMPANIES EXCLUDED FROM THE GPFG*

ANTI-PERSONNEL LAND MINES

Singapore Technologies Engineering (26 April 2002)

PRODUCTION OF CLUSTER MUNITIONS

Textron Inc. (31 December 2008)
Hanwha Corporation (31 December 2007)
Poongsan Corporation (30 November 2006)
Raytheon Co. (31 August 2005)
General Dynamics Corporation (31 August 2005)

PRODUCTION OF NUCLEAR ARMS

Alliant Techsystems Inc. (21 August 2013)
Lockheed Martin Corp. (21 August 2013)
BWX Technologies Inc. (11 January 2013)
Jacobs Engineering Group Inc. (11 January 2013)
Serco Group Plc. (31 December 2007)
Aerojet Rocketdyne Holdings, Inc. (31 December 2007)
Safran S.A. (31 December 2005)
Northrop Grumman Corp. (31 December 2005)
Honeywell International Inc. (31 December 2005)

Airbus Group Finance B.V. (31 December 2005)
Airbus Group N.V. (31 December 2005)
Boeing Co. (31 December 2005)

ACTIONS OR OMISSIONS THAT CONSTITUTE AN UNACCEPTABLE RISK OF THE FUND CONTRIBUTING TO:

Serious or systematic human rights violations

Zuari Agro Chemicals Ltd. (14 October 2013)
Wal-Mart Stores Inc. (31 May 2006)
Wal-Mart de Mexico SA de CV (31 May 2006)

Severe environmental damages

IJM Corp Bhd. (17 August 2015)
Genting Bhd. (17 August 2015)
POSCO (17 August 2015)
Daewoo International Corp. (17 August 2015)
Sesa Sterlite (30 January 2014) (Madras Aluminium Company and Sterlite Industries Ltd. [both excluded 31 October 2007] are merged into Sesa Sterlite)
WTK Holdings Berhad (14 October 2013)
Ta Ann Holdings Berhad (14 October 2013)
Zijin Mining Group (14 October 2013)
Volcan Compaña Minera (14 October 2013)
Lingui Development Berhad Ltd. (16 February 2011)
Samling Global Ltd. (23 August 2010)
Norilsk Nickel (31 October 2009)
Barrick Gold Corp. (30 November 2008)
Rio Tinto Plc. (30 June 2008)
Rio Tinto Ltd. (30 June 2008)

Vedanta Resources Plc. (31 October 2007)
Freeport McMoRan Copper & Gold Inc. (31 May 2006)

GROSS CORRUPTION

ZTE Corporation (7 January 2016)

OTHER PARTICULARLY SERIOUS VIOLATIONS OF FUNDAMENTAL ETHICAL NORMS

San Leon Energy Plc. (4 March 2016)
Potash Corporation of Saskatchewan (6 December 2011)
Elbit Systems Ltd. (31 August 2009)

SERIOUS VIOLATIONS OF THE RIGHTS OF INDIVIDUALS IN SITUATIONS OF WAR OR CONFLICT

Africa Israel Investments (30 January 2014)
Danya Cebus (30 January 2014)
Shikun & Binui Ltd. (31 May 2012)

COMPANIES PLACED UNDER OBSERVATION

Petroleo Brasileiro SA, because of the risk of severe corruption.
Astra International Tbk PT, because of the risk of severe environmental damage.

Source: NBIM, 'Exclusion of Companies', May 2016.

* List excludes twenty-one tobacco companies and fifty-two coal companies.

ACKNOWLEDGMENTS

A decade ago I had the opportunity to work in the newly independent East Timor, an oil-rich country which, through no fault of its own, had a turbulent past. As well as working with some great Timorese colleagues, I met a group of Norwegians who had been sent there by their country's aid agency to provide technical assistance to the government. Some of them had worked in pioneering roles within their own country's oil and gas development, and this experience proved to be very instructive. I especially want to thank Einar Risa, who put me in touch with key people in Norway and gave me a good overview of the key figures in this history.

Upon returning home I wrote about the experience of Norway, and East Timor, in numerous articles for the Australian media. At the time, Australia was going through an unprecedented mining boom, yet there was little discussion about how the country might shepherd the additional revenue over the course of the economic cycle, let alone for future generations. As a result of this work, I met with Norway's ambassador to Australia, Siren Gjerme Eriksen, and after some discussion we came up with the idea of doing some research in Norway. This led to a visit in 2013 during which I conducted a number of the interviews that proved to be the starting point for this book. I want to thank especially First Secretary Kaja Erichsen Glomm, who organised most of the interviews for that visit.

Covering some of the early history proved to be a big challenge but in this regard I was aided by two outstanding academics, Helge Ryggvik and Einar Lie. Also in this regard, I was greatly helped by the Mitchell Library in Sydney, which has an impressive collection of books that cover all facets of Norwegian history, including the oil development. Megan Halsband of the US Library of Congress provided helpful guidance as well. Sverre Dæhlen from the Ministry of Foreign Affairs tracked down valuable archival material. Finn Harald Sandberg, the curator at the Norwegian Petroleum Museum, was very helpful in answering numerous questions and providing background material, while Eldbjørg Vaage Melberg and Jan Bygdevoll from the Norwegian Petroleum Directorate provided many photographs and answered my many questions in a prompt and helpful manner.

Despite researching and writing this book from afar, I was able to track down and interview or correspond with all of the key people who played a role in developing Norway's oil or revenue management policy over the last forty years. Without the cooperation of these people, this book could not have been written. So in this regard I must thank Øystein Olsen, Farouk Al-Kasim, Knut Kjær, Arve Johnsen, Martin Scancke and Petter Nore for the time they have given to me and for answering follow-up questions.

This book would not have happened without the enthusiastic team at Black Inc., especially Chris Feik and Sophy Williams, who secured international publication rights, while editors Nikki Lusk and Jo Rosenberg made many helpful comments. Lastly I must thank my family, and especially Kate, for putting up with long absences and having to listen to me complaining about the difficulties of writing this book. And even my cheeky six-year-old boy made an important contribution. During the writing of the diving chapter he borrowed a library book that mentioned how workers who built the foundations of the Brooklyn Bridge suffered from nitrogen narcosis when they went down below sea level for extended periods.

BIBLIOGRAPHY

Arnold, G., 1978, *Britain's Oil*, Hamish Hamilton, London.

Bang, P. and Thuestad, O., 2014, 'Enforced self regulation in Norway', in Lindøe, P.H. et al. (eds), *Risk Governance of Offshore Oil and Gas Operations*, Cambridge University Press, New York.

Brende, B., 2015, 'The Arctic: important for Norway, important for the world', *Harvard International Review*, 16 July.

Brundtland, G., 2001, 'The annual lecture in the business & the environment programme,' University of Cambridge, 15 March.

Brundtland, G.H., 2002, *Madam PM: A Life in Power and Politics*, Farrar, Straus and Giroux, New York.

Bugg, H.C., 1982, 'A national perspective on the oil blowout problem', in *Managing Technological Accidents: Two Blowouts in the North Sea*, International Institute of Applied Systems Analysis, Oxford, pp. 109–15.

Christou, M. and Konstantinidou, M., 2012, *Safety of Offshore Oil and Gas Operations: Lessons from Past Accident Analysis*, European Commission, Luxembourg.

Crockatt, R., 1994, *The Fifty Years War: The United States and the Soviet Union in World Politics, 1941–1991*, Routledge, London.

Derry, T.K., 1973, *A History of Modern Norway*, Clarendon, Oxford.

Eckbo, P.L., 1981, 'Regulatory intentions and realities: the case of the Norwegian oil industry', in Barker T. and Brailovsky, V. (eds), *Oil or Industry? Energy, Industrialisation and Economic Policy in Canada,*

Mexico, the Netherlands, Norway and the United Kingdom, Academic Press, London, pp. 277–91.

Fischer, D., 1978, 'A decision analysis of the oil blowout at Bravo Platform', IIASA Research Memorandum RM-78-006, Laxenburg, 1 January.

Gjedrem, S., 2001, 'Economic developments and monetary policy in Norway', Speech to the National Council of the Confederation of Norwegian Commercial and Service Enterprises, Oslo, 30 May.

Gjedrem, S., 2010, 'History of economics in Norway' Schweigaard lecture, Governor of Norges Bank, University of Oslo, 23 August.

Gjelsvik, T., 1979, *Norwegian Resistance: 1940–45*, Hurst and Co., London

Gjerde, K.Ø. and Ryggvik, H., 2014, *On the Edge, Under Water: Offshore Diving in Norway*, Wigerstrand, Stavanger.

Gregory, R., 1976, 'Some implications of the growth of the mineral sector', *Australian Journal of Agricultural Economics*, vol. 20, no. 2, August, pp. 71–91.

Hammond, J., 2011, 'The resource curse and oil revenues in Angola and Venezuela', *Science & Society*, vol. 75, no. 3, July, pp. 348–78.

Harsson, B.G. and Preiss, G., 2012, 'Norwegian baselines, maritime boundaries and the UN Convention on the Law of the Sea', *Arctic Review on Law and Politics*, vol. 3, no. 1, pp. 108–29.

Harvie, C., 1994, *Fool's Gold: The Story of North Sea Oil*, Hamish Hamilton, London.

Knutsen, S. and Lie, E., 2002, 'Financial fragility, growth strategies and banking failures: the major Norwegian Banks and the banking crisis, 1987–92', *Business History*, vol. 44, no. 2, pp. 88–111.

Lang, E., 1977, 'The concession laws and Norwegian industrial development', *Scandinavian Journal of History*, vol. 2, nos 1–4, pp. 311, 300.

Lerøen B.J., 1996, *Troll: Gas for Generations*, Statoil, Stavanger.

Lie, E., 2011, 'Wealth in Norwegian', in *On Managing Wealth*, Norges Bank, Oslo.

Lie, E., 2013, 'Learning by failing: the origins of the Norwegian oil fund', unpublished draft paper.

Limbrick, J., 2001, *North Sea Divers: A Requiem*, Authors Online, Herford.

Lind, T. and Mackay G., 1980, *Norwegian Oil Policies*, C. Hurst & Coy, London.

Lindøe. P.H. et al. (eds), 2014, *Risk Governance of Offshore Oil and Gas Operations*, Cambridge University Press, New York.

Listhaug, O., 2007, 'Oil wealth dissatisfaction and political trust', in *Norway in Transition: Transforming a Stable Democracy*, Østerud, Ø. (ed.), Routledge, Abingdon.

Ministry of Finance, 2014, *Fossil-Fuel Investments in the Norwegian Government Pension Fund Global: Addressing Climate Issues Through Exclusion and Active Ownership*, Report by the expert group appointed by the Norwegian Ministry of Finance, Oslo.

Ministry of Finance, 2014, 'Guidelines for observation and exclusion from the Government Pension Fund Global', 18 December.

Ministry of Petroleum and Energy, 2011, *An Industry for the Future: Norway's Petroleum Activities*, Report to Parliament of Norway, Oslo, 28 June.

Ministry of Petroleum and Energy/Norwegian Petroleum Directorate, 2013, *Facts 2013: The Norwegian Petroleum Sector*, NPD, Oslo.

Ministry of Petroleum and Energy/Norwegian Petroleum Directorate, 2014, *Facts 2014: The Norwegian Petroleum Sector*, NPD, Oslo.

Moan, T., 1985, 'The progressive structural failure of the Alexander L. Kielland Platform', in Maier, G., (ed.), *Case Histories in Offshore Engineering*, Springer-Verlag, Wien.

Moan, T., 2010, 'The Alexander Kielland accident: 30 years later', Norwegian Centre of Excellence, www.ntnu.no, viewed 12 February 2015.

Næsheim, T., 1981, *The Alexander L. Kielland Accident,* Report presented to the Ministry of Justice and Police, Norwegian Public Reports, Oslo, vol. 11.

Nelson, B., 1991, *State Offshore: Petroleum, Politics, and State Intervention on the British and Norwegian Continental Shelves*, Praeger, New York.

Nore, P, 1979. 'The Norwegian state's relationship to the international oil companies over North Sea oil 1965–75', PhD thesis, Thames Polytechnic.

Norske Oljemuseum, 2011, *Oil and Gas Fields in Norway*, Norske Oljemuseum, Stavanger.

Norwegian Oil Museum, *Oil and Gas Fields in Norway – Industrial Heritage Plan*, 2010, Stavanger.

Norwegian Oil Museum, *Oil and Gas Fields in Norway – Troll Area*, 2011, Stavanger.

Norwegian Petroleum Directorate, 2012, *Norwegian Continental Shelf, Special Report*, No. 2, Stavanger.

Olsen, Ø., 2013, 'Monetary policy and wealth management in a small petroleum economy', Presentation to Harvard Kennedy School, 9 April.

Olsen, Ø., 2014, 'Economic perspectives', Address to the Supervisory Council of Norges Bank and invited guests, Norges Bank, Oslo, 12 February.

Olsen, Ø., 2015, 'Managing Norway's oil wealth', Speech at the *Desemberkonferansen* oil and gas conference in Kristiansund, Norges Bank, Oslo, 3 December.

Olsen, Ø., 2016, 'Economic perspectives', Address to the Supervisory Council of Norges Bank and invited guests, Norges Bank, Oslo, 18 February.

Petroleum Safety Authority, 2014, *Safety Signals and Status*, Stavanger.

Rich, N., 2013, 'Diving deep into danger', *The New York Review of Books*, 7 February.

Ross, M., 2012, *The Oil Curse: How Petroleum Wealth Shapes the Development of Nations*, Princeton University Press, Princeton.

Ryggvik, H., 2010, *The Norwegian Oil Experience: A Toolbox for*

Managing Resources? Centre for Technology, Innovation and Culture, University of Oslo.

Ryggvik, H., 2013, *Building a Skilled National Offshore Oil Industry: The Norwegian Experience*, NHO, Oslo.

Ryggvik, H., 2014, 'Inspections, independence and intelligence', in Lindøe. P.H. et al. (eds), *Risk Governance of Offshore Oil and Gas Operations,* Cambridge University Press, New York.

Skancke, M., 2003, 'Fiscal policy and petroleum fund management in Norway', in *Fiscal Policy Formulation and Implementation in Oil-Producing Countries,* IMF, Washington, pp. 318–20.

Sjavik, J., 2008, *The Historical Dictionary of Norway*, Scarecrow Press, Lanhan.

Smith, Norman J., 2011, *The Sea of Lost Opportunity: North Sea Oil and Gas, British Industry and the Offshore Supplies Office*, Elsevier, Oxford.

Stevens P. and Dietsche E., 2008, 'Resource curse: an analysis of causes, experiences and possible ways forward', *Energy Policy*, vol. 36, pp. 56–65.

Sunley, E.M., Baunsgaard, T. and Simard, D., 2003, 'Revenue from the oil and gas sector: issues and country experience', in Davis, J.M., Ossowski, R. and Fedelino, A. (eds), *Fiscal Policy Formulation and Implementation in Oil-Producing Countries*, IMF, Washington.

Sutton, M., 1984, 'Structuralism: the Latin American record and the new critique', in Killick, T. (ed.), *The IMF and Stabilisation, Developing Country Experiences*, Heinemann, London, pp. 19–68.

Taylor, S.J., 2005, *Oilwork: North Sea Diaries,* Birlinn, Edinburgh.

Thurber, M.C., Hults, D.R. and Heller, P.R., 2011, 'Exporting the "Norwegian Model": the effect of administrative design on oil', *Energy Policy*, vol. 39, pp. 5366–78.

Thurber, M. and Instad, B., 2012, 'Norway's evolving champion: Statoil and the politics of state enterprise', in Victor, D., Hults, D. and Thurber, M. (eds), *Oil and Governance: State-Owned Enterprises and the World Energy Supply*, Cambridge University Press, Cambridge, pp. 599–655.

Todnem, K. et al., 1991, 'Neurological long-term consequences of deep diving', *British Journal of Industrial Medicine*, vol. 48, pp. 258–66.

United Nations, 1958, 'Convention on the Continental Shelf', United Nations Treaty Collection, Geneva.

United States Government, 1945, *Proclamation 2667 – Policy of the United States with Respect to the Natural Resources of the Subsoil and Sea Bed of the Continental Shelf*, http://www.presidency.ucsb.edu/ws/?pid=12332.

Wertz, W.C. (ed.), 1983, *Phillips: The First Sixty-Six Years*, Phillips Petroleum, Bartlesville.

Yergin, D., 1992, *The Prize*, Touchstone, New York.

NOTES

1. Author interview with Einar Lie, 15 January 2015.

2. *The Financial Times*, 'Room for companies to negotiate', 11 December 1974.

3. *The Financial Times*, 'Oil companies may quit if Norway introduces tax', 6 December 1974.

4. *The Financial Times*, 'Government takes first step towards North Sea tax', 20 November 1947.

5. Author interview with Einar Lie, 15 January 2015.

6. Ross, M., *The Oil Curse: How Petroleum Wealth Shapes the Development of Nations*, Princeton University Press, Princeton, 2012, pp. 1–5.

7. All dollar figures are US dollars unless otherwise indicated.

8. Author interview with deputy finance minister Kjetil Lund, June 2013. Figures confirmed in statement to the author by Ministry of Finance official Dorte Frange, 12 May 2016.

9. Government of Canada, 'Key facts and figures on the natural resources sector', www.nrcan.gc.ca/publications/key-facts/16013, 2015.

10. Alberta Heritage Savings Trust Fund, *Second Quarter 2015–2016*, 2016, p. 1.

11. ABS, *Net international investment position*, cat. no. 5302.0, 11 May 2016.

12. Population statistics: statisticsnorway.no, Table 05803; Malthus's remarks: Olsen, Ø., 'Economic perspectives', Address to the Supervisory Council of Norges Bank and invited guests, 13 February 2014, p. 2.

13. Lie, E., 'Wealth in Norwegian', in *On Managing Wealth*, Norges Bank, Oslo, 2011, p. 26.

14. Olsen, 'Economic perspectives', p. 10.

15. Ryggvik, H., *The Norwegian Oil Experience: A Toolbox for Managing Resources?* Centre for Technology, Innovation and Culture, University of Oslo, 2010, p. 56.

16. www.telegraph.co.uk/culture/9354262/Edvard-Munch-The-Modern-Eye-Tate-Modern-review.html, viewed 5 June 2016.

17. Lang, E., 'The concession laws and Norwegian industrial development', *Scandinavian Journal of History*, vol. 2, nos 1–4, 1977, p. 311.

18. Gjelsvik, T., *Norwegian Resistance: 1940–45*, Hurst and Co., London, 1979, p. 118.

19. *The Telegraph*, 'Gunnar Sonsteby', 10 May 2012.

20. Gjelsvik, p. 128.

21. Derry, T.K., *A History of Modern Norway*, Clarendon, Oxford, 1973, p. 400.

22. Nore, P., 'The Norwegian state's relationship to the international oil companies over North Sea oil 1965–75', PhD thesis, Thames Polytechnic, 1979, p. 22.

23. ibid., p. 21.

24. ibid., p. 22.

25. *The New York Times*, 'Jens Christian Hauge, guide of modern Norway, dies at 91', 4 November 2006.

26. 'Proclamation 2667 – policy of the United States with respect to the natural resources of the subsoil and sea bed of the Continental Shelf', www.presidency.ucsb.edu/ws/?pid=12332, viewed 1 August 2014.

27. American Oil and Gas Historical Society, 'Offshore petroleum history', aoghs.org/offshore-history/offshore-oil-history/, viewed 28 July 2014.

28. United Nations, 'Convention on the Continental Shelf', Geneva, 29 April 1958.

29. Lind, T. and Mackay, G., *Norwegian Oil Policies*, C. Hurst & Coy, London, 1980, p. 5.

30. Nore, p. 6.

31. Nelson, B., *State Offshore: Petroleum, Politics, and State Intervention on the British and Norwegian Continental Shelves*, Praeger, New York, 1991, p. 14.

32. Wertz, W.C. (ed.), *Phillips: The First Sixty-Six Years*, Phillips Petroleum, Bartlesville, 1983, p. 8.

33. Ryggvik, 2010, p. 11.

34. Ministry of Petroleum and Energy, 'Oil and gas', www.regjeringen. no/en/dep/oed/Subject/oil-and-gas/norways-oil-history-in-5-minutes.html?id=440538, viewed 19 July 2014.

35. 'Royal Decree of 31 May 1963 relating to the sovereignty of Norway over the sea-bed and subsoil outside the Norwegian coast', www.un.org/depts/los/LEGISLATIONANDTREATIES/PDFFILES/NOR_1963_Decree.pdf, viewed 12 May 2016.

36. Nore, p.6.

37. Ryggvik, 2010, p. 9.

38. United Kingdom Government, Aide-Mémoire, Norwegian Ministry of Foreign Affairs Archive, 18 February 1964, p. 1.

39. *The Economist*, 'Putting the Union Jack on the shelf', 30 November 1963.

40. Author's personal communication with Ministry of Foreign Affairs spokesperson, 5 August 2014.

41. Nelson, p. 93.

42. *The Economist*, 'Another piece in the North Sea puzzle', 28 August 1965.

43. NPD, 'In at the start', *A Journal from the Norwegian Petroleum Directorate*, vol. 1, NPD, Stavanger, 2015, p. 10.

44. ibid., p. 12.

45. NPD, 'Found his field', *A Journal from the Norwegian Petroleum Directorate*, vol. 1, NPD, Stavanger, 2015, p. 14.

46. Ryggvik, 2010, p. 18.

47. ibid., p. 21.

48. Nelson, p. 28.

49. Author interview with Farouk Al-Kasim, 21 September 2015.

50. ibid.

51. ibid.

52. Nelson, p. 30. Nelson draws from an account written by Norwegian author and former newspaper editor Egil Helle, *Norges Olje*.

53. Yergin, D., *The Prize*, Touchstone, New York, 1992, p. 668.

54. NPD, 'In at the start', p. 12.

55. ibid.

56. *GeoExPro*, 'First commercial North Sea discovery', February 2011, p. 47.

57. Author's personal communication with Finn Sandberg, curator of the Norwegian Oil Museum, 25 September 2015.

58. Author interview with Farouk Al-Kasim, 21 September 2015.

59. Author's personal communication with Finn Sandberg.

60. The reserves totalled 569 million cubic metres of oil and 164 billion cubic metres of gas: Norwegian Petroleum Directorate/Ministry of Petroleum and Energy, *Facts 2013: The Norwegian Petroleum Sector*, Oslo, 2013, p. 71.

61. Olsen, Ø., 'Managing Norway's oil wealth', Speech at the *Desemberkonferansen* oil and gas conference in Kristiansund, 3 December 2015; Norwegian Petroleum Directorate/Ministry of Petroleum and Energy, *Facts 2014*, 2014, p. 69.

62. Olsen, 2014, p. 2.

63. Sjavik, J., *The Historical Dictionary of Norway*, Scarecrow Press, Lanhan, 2008, p. xxi.

64. Ryggvik, 2010, p. 15.

65. ibid., p. 14.

66. ibid., p. 13.

67. Author interview with Petter Nore, 3 February 2016.

68. Lind and Mackay, pp. 102–3.

69. Author interview with Einar Risa, 13 February 2014.

70. Harvie, C., *Fool's Gold: The Story of North Sea Oil*, Hamish Hamilton, London, 1994, p. 146.

71. Smith, Norman J., *The Sea of Lost Opportunity: North Sea oil and Gas, British Industry and the Offshore Supplies Office*, Elsevier, Oxford, 2011, p. 120.

72. Department of State, Cable from London to Washington, 21 May 1973.

73. Department of State, Cable from Oslo to Washington, 18 July 1975.

74. Author interview with Einar Lie, 15 January 2015.

75. Author interview with Trond Giske, industry minister, June 2013.

76. Department of State, Cable from Oslo to Washington, 18 July 1975.

77. Author interview with Gunvor Ulstein, June 2013.

78. Ministry of Petroleum and Energy, *An Industry for the Future – Norway's Petroleum Activities*, Report to Parliament, 24 June 2011, p. 8.

79. Lind and Mackay, pp. 19–20.

80. Ryggvik, H., *Building a Skilled National Offshore Oil Industry – The Norwegian Experience*, NHO, Oslo, 2013, p. 23.

81. Ryggvik, 2010, p. 25.

82. Krone-dollar conversions based on the Norges Bank's annual exchange rate records.

83. *Financial Times*, 'Oil in troubled waters', 3 January 1974.

84. Lind and Mackay, p. 109.

85. ibid., p. 101.

86. Lerøen, B., *Troll: Gas for Generations*, Statoil, 1996, pp. 46–7.

87. NPD/MPE, 2013, p. 93.

88. Ryggvik. 2010, p. 42.

89. Nelson, p. 40.

90. Author interview with Petter Nore, 3 February 2016.

91. Lind and Mackay, p. 31.

92. ibid., p. 35.

93. ibid., p. 101.

94. ibid., p. 45.

95. Harvie, pp. 17–18.

96. Smith, pp. 69–71.

97. Lind and Mackay, p. 30.

98. Lind and Mackay, p. 31.

99. Eckbo, P.L., 'Regulatory intentions and realities: the case of the Norwegian oil industry', in Barker, T., and Brailovsky, V. (eds), *Oil or Industry? Energy, Industrialisation and Economic Policy in Canada, Mexico, the Netherlands, Norway and the United Kingdom*, Academic Press, London, 1981, p. 280.

100. Author interview with Petter Nore, 3 February 2016.

101. First told to the author by Einar Risa in January 2014 interview. Confirmed in personal communication with Arve Johnsen, 14 October 2015.

102. Smith, pp. 48–9.

103. Author interview with Einar Hangeland, 10 November 2014.

104. Author's personal communication with Arve Johnsen, 14 October 2015.

105. Lind and Mackay, p. 39.

106. Author's personal communication with Arve Johnsen, 14 October 2015.

107. Ryggvik, 2010, p. 29.

108. Moan, T., 'The Alexander Kielland accident: 30 years later', Norwegian Centre of Excellence www.ntnu.no, 2010, viewed 12 February 2015.

109. Only 2 per cent of the Norwegian mainland is considered arable.

110. Ryggvik, 2013, pp. 58–9.

111. Norske Oljemuseum, *Oil and Gas Fields in Norway*, Norske Oljemuseum, Stavanger, 2011, p. 130.

112. Wertz, 1983, p. 175.

113. Author interview with Hans Klasson, 21 September 2015.

114. Bugg, H.C., 'A national perspective on the oil blowout problem', in *Managing Technological Accidents: Two Blowouts in the North Sea*, International Institute of Applied Systems Analysis, Oxford, 1982, p. 111.

115. 'How it began', Petroleum Safety Authority Norway, http://www.psa. no/our-history/category1201.html, viewed 16 September 2013.

116. Thurber, M.C., Hults, D.R. and Heller, P.R., 'Exporting the "Norwegian Model": the effect of administrative design on oil sector performance', *Energy Policy*, vol. 39, fn. 21, 2011, p. 5371

117. Ryggvik, H., 'Inspections, independence and intelligence', in Lindøe. P.H. et al. (eds), *Risk Governance of Offshore Oil and Gas Operations*, Cambridge University Press, New York, 2014, p. 388.

118. Lind and Mackay, p. 39.

119. Brundtland, G.H., *Madam PM: A Life in Power and Politics*, Farrar, Straus and Giroux, New York, 2002, p. 94.

120. Fischer, D., 'A decision analysis of the oil blowout at Bravo Platform', IIASA Research Memorandum RM-78-006, Laxenburg, January 1978, pp. 1–2.

121. National Oceanic and Atmospheric Administration, 'Incident news – Ekofisk Bravo oil field', incidentnews.noaa.gov/incident/ 6237, viewed 14 April 2014.

122. Brundtland, G., 'The annual lecture in the business & the environment programme', University of Cambridge, 15 March 2001.

123. Brundtland, 2002, p. 96.

124. Fischer, p. 20.

125. Brundtland, 2002, p. 97.

126. Fischer, p. 21.

127. Brundtland, 2002, p. 99.

128. Bugg, p. 113.

129. Arnold, G., *Britain's Oil*, Hamish Hamilton, London, 1978, p. 22.

130. Kielland, A.L., *Garman and Worse*, 1880, quoted in Olsen. Ø., 'Economic perspectives', Annual address by Mr Øystein Olsen, Governor of the Norges Bank (Central Bank of Norway), to the Supervisory Council of Norges Bank, Norges Bank, Oslo, 12 February 2015.

131. Næsheim, T., *The Alexander L. Kielland accident,* Report presented to the Ministry of Justice and Police, Norwegian Public Reports, Oslo, vol. 11, 1981, pp. 32–3.

132. ibid., p. 36.

133. ibid., pp. 371–2; Moan, T., 'The progressive structural failure of the Alexander L. Kielland platform', in Maier, G., (ed.), *Case Histories in Offshore Engineering*, Springer-Verlag, Wien, 1985, p. 2.

134. *Aftenposten*, 'Da olje-eventyret kostet 123 liv', 26 March 2010.

135. Christou, M. and Konstantinidou, M., *Safety of Offshore Oil and Gas Operations: Lessons from Past Accident Analysis*, European Commission, Luxembourg, 2012, p. 16.

136. Næsheim, p. 229.

137. ibid., p. 136.

138. *The Sun-Herald*, 'Hero Mike took the icy plunge', 30 March 1980.

139. Næsheim, p. 136.

140. *Aftenposten*, 210.

141. Gjerde, K.Ø. and Ryggvik, H., *On the Edge, Under Water: Offshore Diving in Norway*, Wigerstrand, Stavanger, 2014, p. 194.

142. Næsheim, pp. 227–8.

143. Gjerde and Ryggvik, p. 201.

144. ibid., p. 200.

145. Bang, P. and Thuestad, O., 'Enforced self-regulation in Norway', in Lindøe. P.H. et al. (eds), *Risk Governance of Offshore Oil and Gas Operations*, Cambridge University Press, New York, 2014, p. 249.

146. ibid., p. 251.

147. ibid., p. 255.

148. Næsheim, p. 235.

149. *The Guardian*, 'Piper Alpha disaster: how 167 oil rig workers died', 5 July 2003.

150. Author's personal communication with Arve Johnsen, 13 October 2015.

151. www.history.com/topics/brooklyn-bridge, viewed 11 January 2016.

152. Rich, N., 'Diving deep into danger', *The New York Review of Books*, 7 February 2013.

153. Gjerde and Ryggvik, p. 47.

154. Gjerde and Ryggvik, pp. 54–5.

155. Author interview with Alan Krell, 20 April 2015.

156. Limbrick, J., *North Sea Divers: A Requiem*, Authors Online, Herford, 2001.

157. Author's personal communication with HSE senior media officer Jason Green, 28 March 2015.

158. Gjerde and Ryggvik, p. 95.

159. ibid., p. 119.

160. ibid., p. 129.

161. BBC, 'Norway's underwater "guinea pigs"', 27 May 2008, news.bbc. co.uk/2/hi/uk_news/magazine/7314283.stm, viewed 18 October 2015.

162. Gjerde and Ryggvik, p. 138.

163. Author's personal communication with Arve Johnsen, 13 October 2015.

164. Gjerde and Ryggvik, pp. 177, 181.

165. Statistics Norway, *Yearbook, 2013*, 2013.

166. Gjerde and Ryggvik, pp. 203–6.

167. NPD/MPE 2014, 2013 data, p. 74.

168. Gjerde and Ryggvik, p. 84.

169. Ryggvik, 2014, p. 93.

170. Author interview with Angus Kleppe, 22 April 2015.

171. Ricket, O., 'Norway's North Sea divers lost their minds over oil', www.vice.com, 4 August 2014.

172. Author's personal communication with Kristin Øye Gjerde, 29 January 2016.

173. ibid.

174. Author interview with Alan Krell, 20 April 2015.

175. Author interview with Norman Smith, 13 October 2015.

176. Gjerde and Ryggvik, p. 300.

177. Todnem, K. et al., 'Neurological long-term consequences of deep diving', *British Journal of Industrial Medicine*, vol. 48, 1991, pp. 258–66.

178. Report to the Storting, no. 47 (2002–03).

179. Author's personal communication with a spokesperson for the ministry, 8 May 2015.

180. *The Financial Times*, 'Room for companies to negotiate', 11 December 1974.

179. US State Department, 'Stiff new Norwegian excess profits tax on oil companies', Cable from Oslo to Washington, 10 December 1974.

180. US State Department, 'Amoco', Cable from Oslo embassy to Washington, 19 March 1975.

181. ibid.

182. Briefing note for director-general of Ministry of Finance, 13 December 1974, Ministry of Foreign Affairs archive.

183. Lind and Mackay, p. 121.

184. www.regjeringen.no/en/topics/energy/oil-and-gas/petroleum-price-board-and-the-norm-price/id661459/, viewed 2 December 2015.

185. Nelson, fn 44.

186. *The Financial Times*, 'Government takes first step towards North Sea tax', 20 November 1974.

187. *The Financial Times*, 'North Sea oil tax fixed at 45%', 20 February 1975.

188. Sunley, E.M., Baunsgaard, T and Simard, D., 'Revenue from the oil and gas sector: issues and country experience', in Davis, J.M. Ossowski, R. and Fedelino, A., *Fiscal Policy Formulation and Implementation in Oil-Producing Countries*, IMF, Washington, 2003, p. 178.

189. Author interview with Øystein Olsen, 6 June 2013.

190. Lind and Mackay, p. 25.

191. Lie, E., 'Learning by failing: the origins of the Norwegian oil fund', unpublished draft paper, 2013, p. 11.

192. Author interview with Petter Nore, 3 February 2016.

193. Lie, pp. 12–13.

194. ibid., p. 12.

195. ibid.

196. Knutsen, S. and Lie, E., 'Financial fragility, growth strategies and banking failures: the major Norwegian banks and the banking crisis, 1987–92', *Business History*, vol. 44, no. 2, 2002, p. 93.

197. ibid., p. 96.

198. ibid., p. 93.

199. Lie, p. 16.

200. ibid.

201. *The Calgary Herald*, '"Alberta should copy Alberta on oil royalties," says former Norwegian finance minister', 4 June 2015.

202. Author interview with Martin Skancke, 3 November 2015.

203. Skancke, M., 'Fiscal policy and petroleum fund management in Norway', in *Fiscal Policy Formulation and Implementation in Oil-Producing Countries*, IMF, Washington, 2003, pp. 318–20.

204. Lie, pp. 3–10.

205. ibid., p. 16.

206. Office for National Statistics, *Labour Market Trends*, 1996, p. 6.

207. National Archives, 'Sterling devalued and the IMF loan', www.nationalarchives.gov.uk/cabinetpapers/themes/sterling-devalued-imf-loan.htm, viewed 12 November 2015.

208. Author interview with Norman Smith, 13 October 2015.

209. *The Economist*, 'The New Vikings', 26 July 1975.

210. Author interview with Norman Smith, 13 October 2015.

211. Ryggvik, 2013, p. 32.

212. *The Economist*, 'The New Vikings'.

213. Ryggvik, 2013, p. 33.

214. Norwegian Oil Museum, *Oil and Gas Fields in Norway – Industrial Heritage Plan*, Norwegian Oil Museum, Stavanger, 2010, pp. 131–3.

215. Yergin, p. 669.

216. Ryggvik, 2013, p. 53.

217. ibid., p. 74.

218. NPD, *Norwegian Continental Shelf, Special Report*, no. 2, NPD, Stavanger, 2012, p. 13.

219. Crockatt, R., *The Fifty Years War: The United States and the Soviet Union in World Politics, 1941–1991*, Routledge, London, 1994, p. 311.

220. 'East-west economic relations and Poland-related sanctions', National security decision, directive no. 66, 29 November 1982, www.reagan.utexas.edu/archives/reference/Scanned%20NSDDs/ NSDD66.pdf, viewed 6 September 2015.

221. Lerøen, p. 81.

222. ibid.

223. *The New York Times*, 'Reagan lifts sanctions on sales for Soviet pipeline; reports accord with Allies', 14 November 1982.

224. NPD, 2012, p. 13.

225. ibid., p.17.

226. CIA, *The World Factbook*, 2015, www.cia.gov/library/publications/ the-world-factbook/fields/2250.html, viewed 12 September 2015.

227. NPD, 2012, p. 16.

228. ibid., p. 14.

229. Norwegian Oil Museum, 'Troll area', *Oil and Gas Fields in Norway*, Norwegian Oil Museum, Stavanger, 2011, p. 153.

230. Ryggvik, 2013, p. 68.

231. Lerøen, pp. 45–6.

232. Ryggvik, 2013, p. 101.

233. Author's personal communication with Arve Johnsen, 14 October 2015.

234. Statoil, 'Statoil and Rosneft move forward with exploration cooperation', Press release, 13 June 2013.

235. Norwegian Oil Museum, 2011, p. 155.

236. Gjerde and Ryggvik, p. 268.

237. *The New York Times*, 'Huge gas rig begins journey in Norway', 11 May 1995, p. D8.

238. Lerøen, p. 84.

239. Lerøen, p. 87.

240. Norwegian Government Petroleum Fund, *Annual Report*, Norges Bank, Oslo, 1998, p. 17.

241. NPD/MPE, 2014, p. 62.

242. Author interview with Martin Skancke, 3 November 2015.

243. Author interview with Knut Kjær, 16 October 2015.

244. Author interview with Martin Skancke, 3 November 2015.

245. Norwegian Government Petroleum Fund, 1998, p. 4.

246. Norwegian Biographical Dictionary, (*Norsk biografisk leksikon*), nbl.snl.no/Svein_Gjedrem, viewed 6 October 2014.

247. Norwegian Government Petroleum Fund, 1998, p. 4.

248. NBIM, *Annual Report*, Norges Bank, Oslo, 2007, p. 76.

249. Norwegian Government Petroleum Fund, *Annual Report*, Norges Bank, Oslo, 1999, p. 21.

250. NBIM, 2007, p. 76.

251. Slyngstad, Y., 'Introductory statement before the Standing Committee on Finance and Economic Affairs of the Storting', NBIM, Oslo, 29 April 2016.

252. Author's personal communication via spokesperson Martha Skaar, 11 May 2016.

253. Author interview with Knut Kjær, 16 October 2015.

254. NBIM, *GPFG Quarterly Report*, NBIM, Oslo, March 2016, p. 7.

255. NPD/MPE, 2014, p. 63.

256. Author interview with Øystein Olsen, 6 June 2013.

257. Gjedrem, S., 'Economic developments and monetary policy in Norway', Speech to the National Council of the Confederation of

Norwegian Commercial and Service Enterprises, Oslo, 30 May 2001, p. 1.

258. ibid., p.2.

259. Gjedrem, S., 'History of economics in Norway' Schweigaard lecture, University of Oslo, 23 August 2010, p. 7.

260. Author interview with Hilde Singsaas, June 2015.

261. Author interview with Liv Nordhaug, July 2013.

262. *The Economist*, 'Norwegian blues', 10 October 2015.

263. IMF, *Article IV Consultation*, Washington, 2015, p. 13.

264. *The Financial Times*, 'Norwegian bank governor calls for fiscal rule change', 26 February 2012.

265. *News in English*, 'Reaction mixed to spending cut call, 12 August 2012.

266. Author interview with Knut Kjær, 16 October 2015.

267. Author interview with Martin Skancke, 3 November 2015.

268. Olsen, Ø., 2015.

269. Author interview with Ketil Solvik-Olsen, 12 June 2013.

270. Olsen, Ø., 2015.

271. Olsen, Ø., 2016.

272. Olsen, Ø., 2015.

273. NBIM, 'Council on Ethics – History', etikkradet.no/en/history/, viewed 2 December 2015.

274. ibid.

275. Author's personal communication with Hans Olav Syversen, 27 January 2016.

276. Ministry of Finance, *Fossil-fuel investments in the Norwegian Government Pension Fund Global: Addressing Climate Issues through Exclusion and Active Ownership*, Report by the expert group appointed by the Norwegian ministry of finance, Ministry of Finance, Oslo, 2014, p. 4.

277. Ministry of Finance, 'Guidelines for observation and exclusion from the Government Pension Fund Global', Ministry of Finance, Oslo, 18 December 2014.

278. Minister of Finance, Press release, 10 April 2015.

279. Parliament of Norway, Press release, 28 May 2015.

280. *The Financial Times*, 'Norway oil fund chief jettisons passivity', 9 August 2015.

281. NBIM, *Responsible Investment – Government Pension Fund Global*, NBIM, Oslo, 2015, p. 44.

282. ibid., p. 24.

283. ibid., p. 67.

284. Statistics Norway, 'General government, financial assets and liabilities, 2014', 26 November 2015.

285. Statistics Norway, *Yearbook 2013*, p. 265.

286. Statistics Norway, 'Foreign assets and liabilities, Q3 2015,' 3 December 2015.

287. NPD/MPE, 2014, p. 22.

288. Ministry of Foreign Affairs, 'Climate change in the Arctic a warning for the rest of the world', Media release, 7 December 2015.

289. Brende, B., 'The Arctic: important for Norway, important for the world', *Harvard International Review*, 16 April 2015.

290. Author interview with Ane Hansdatter Kismul, June 2013.

291. NPD, 'Found his field', p. 15.

292. Harsson, B.G. and Preiss, G., 'Norwegian baselines, maritime boundaries and the UN Convention on the Law of the Sea', *Arctic Review on Law and Politics*, vol. 3, no. 1, 2012, p. 126.

293. Hughes, E., 'Karl Ove Knausgaard became a literary sensation by exposing his every secret', *New Republic*, 8 April 2014.

294. *The Guardian*, 'Karl Ove Knausgård condemns Norway's Arctic oil plans', 19 May 2015.

295. Petroleum Safety Authority, *Safety Signals and Status*, PSA, Stavanger, 2014, p. 8.

296. ibid., p. 18.

297. ibid., p. 5.

298. Author interview with Tord Lien, 27 February 2015.

299. Ryggvik, 2010, p. 109.

300. Author interview with Anne Myhrvold, 12 August 2015.

301. Author interview with Finn Carlsen, 12 August 2015.

302. Statoil, 'Seeking new acreage on the NCS', Press release, 3 December 2015.

303. Author's personal communication with Statoil company spokesperson, 7 December 2015.

304. Government of Norway, 'Announcement 23rd licensing round awards', Press release, 18 May 2016.

305. Wood Mackenzie, Media release, 7 December 2015.

306. Author interview with Pål Haremo, 9 April 2014.

307. Author interview with Øystein Olsen, 6 June 2013.

308. Olsen, Ø., 'Monetary policy and wealth management in a small petroleum economy', Presentation to Harvard Kennedy School, 9 April 2013, slide 2.

309. Norges Bank, Press release, 12 November 2015.

310. IMF, p. 9.

311. Ryggvik, 2010, p. 112.

312. Author's personal communication with Helge Ryggvik, 1 December 2015.

313. International Energy Agency, 'Statistics: Search statistics by country', 2013, www.iea.org.

314. Author interview with Tord Lien, 27 February 2015.

315. The peak production level was 181 million standard cubic metres oil equivalent (sm³o.e).

316. International Energy Agency, 'IEA Energy Atlas', IEA, 2015.

317. The overall petroleum production peak was 261 million sm³o.e, or 1.6 billion barrels of oil equivalent.

318. MPE/NPD, 2014, p. 13.

319. International Energy Agency, *World Energy Outlook*, 2014, p. 147.

320. MPE/NPD, 2014, p. 25.

321. Author's personal communication with NPD spokesperson, 2 December 2015.

322. BP, www.bp.com/en/global/corporate/energy-economics/statistical-review-of-world-energy.html, 2015, viewed 8 December 2015.

323. BP, *Statistical Review Data Workbook*, 'Oil production – barrels', 2015.

324. Olsen, Ø., 2015.

325. Author interview with Pål Helsing, 27 February 2015.

326. Ryggvik, 2013, p. 129.

327. Author interview with Lien, 27 February 2015.

328. Author interview with Trond Liavaag, 5 June 2013.

INDEX